Substitute Teaching?

Everything you need to get the students on your side and teach them too!
Ready-to-use tools, tips, and lesson ideas for every grade from K–8

AMANDA YUILL

Pembroke Publishers Limited

© 2016 Pembroke Publishers
538 Hood Road
Markham, Ontario, Canada L3R 3K9
www.pembrokepublishers.com

Distributed in the U.S. by Stenhouse Publishers
480 Congress Street
Portland, ME 04101
www.stenhouse.com

Library and Archives Canada Cataloguing in Publication

Yuill, Amanda, author
    Substitute teaching? : everything you need to get the students on your side and teach them too! Ready-to-use tools, tips, and lesson ideas for every grade from K-8 / Amanda Yuill.

Issued in print and electronic formats.
ISBN 978-1-55138-312-5 (paperback).--ISBN 978-1-55138-914-1 (pdf)

    1. Substitute teaching. 2. Classroom management. 3. Education, Elementary--Activity programs. 4. Early childhood education--Activity programs. I. Title.

LB2844.1.S8Y94 2016   371.14'122   C2016-900005-2
                                              C2016-900006-0

Editor: Kat Mototsune
Cover Design: John Zehethofer
Typesetting: Jay Tee Graphics Ltd.

Printed and bound in Canada
9 8 7 6 5 4 3 2 1

MIX
Paper from
responsible sources
FSC® C004071

Contents

Introduction   7

Chapter 1: Toolkit for Substitute Teaching   9

The First Ten Minutes: Getting Their Attention   9
Bag of Tools for Keeping Their Attention (and Staying Sane)   10
   Incentives/Rewards   11
   Games   12
   Magic   12
   Jokes (in Case You're Not Funny)   13
   Gross Facts   13
   Scary Stories that Won't Cause Nightmares   13
   Funny Stories   14
   All About You   14
Classroom Management, NOT Babysitting   15
   Attendance   15
   Students Who Make You Earn Your Pay   15
   Please, Stop Talking!   16
   There's No Playing Tag Inside   16
   Getting Students to Do Their Work   17
   Recess Problems—Not Your Problem   18
   To Call or Not to Call—the Office   18
Finding Your Own Style   19

Chapter 2: A Typical Day Substitute Teaching: An Oxymoron   21

Before Students Arrive   21
   Finding the School   21
   Finding the Classroom   21
   Being Flexible   21
   Finding the Day Plans—or Not   22
   Last-Minute Preparation   23
With Students   23
   Enter the Students   23
   Self-Introduction and Attendance   23
   Classroom Routines   23
   Doing the Work the Teacher Left   24
   Yard/Hall/Lunchroom Duty   25
   Dismissal   25

Chapter 3: Substitute Teaching Kindergarten   27

Help! The Kindergarten Kids Are Eating Me!   27
What Kindergarten Students Are Like   27
   Physically   27
   Socially   28

Academically   *29*
How to Teach Kindergarten Well   *29*
Kindergarten Day Plan and Lessons   *31*
Extra Activities and Games   *37*

Chapter 4: Substitute Teaching Primary Grades   *43*

Grade 1: Can I Hold Your Hand?   *43*
   What Grade 1 Students Are Like   *43*
   How to Teach Grade 1 Well   *45*
Grade 2: I'm Not Your Friend!   *46*
   What Grade 2 Students Are Like   *46*
   How to Teach Grade 2 Well   *48*
Grade 3: That's Not Fair!   *48*
   What Grade 3 Students Are Like   *48*
   How to Teach Grade 3 Well   *49*
Primary Day Plan and Lessons   *50*
Extra Activities and Games   *57*
   Grade 1   *58*
   Grade 2   *58*
   Grade 3   *59*

Chapter 5: Substitute Teaching Junior Grades   *71*

Grade 4: They Can Finally Tie Their Shoelaces   *71*
   What Grade 4 Students Are Like   *71*
   How to Teach Grade 4 Well   *72*
Grade 5: They're So Nice   *73*
   What Grade 5 Students Are Like   *73*
   How to Teach Grade 5 Well   *74*
Grade 6: Spring Fever!   *75*
   What Grade 6 Students Are Like   *75*
   How to Teach Grade 6 Well   *76*
Junior Day Plan and Lessons   *77*
Extra Activities and Games   *86*
   Grade 4   *86*
   Grade 5   *86*
   Grade 6   *87*

Chapter 6: Substitute Teaching Intermediate Grades   *101*

Grade 7: Kids and Hormones   *101*
   What Grade 7 Students Are Like   *101*
   How to Teach Grade 7 Well   *102*
Grade 8: King of the Hill   *103*
   What Grade 8 Students Are Like   *103*
   How to Teach Grade 8 Well   *104*
Intermediate Day Plan and Lessons   *105*
Extra Activities and Games   *111*
   Grade 7   *111*
   Grade 8   *112*

Chapter 7: Substitute Teaching Beyond the Three Rs   *127*

French: Parlez-Vous Francais? Non?   *127*
   Tips for Teaching French   *127*
   Lesson Plan   *127*
Physical Education: Don't Hit Him in the Head with the Ball!   *129*
   Tips for Teaching Phys Ed   *130*
   Lesson Plan   *130*
Music: Please Don't Make Me Sing!   *132*
   Tips for Teaching Music   *132*
   Lesson Plan   *133*
Dance: Jump, Jump Around!   *134*
   Tips for Teaching Dance   *134*
   Lesson Plan   *134*
Drama: Haven't I Had Enough Drama Today?   *136*
   Tips for Teaching Drama   *136*
   Lesson Plan   *137*
Art: No, You Can't Use the Scissors to Cut Your Hair!   *138*
   Tips for Teaching Art   *138*
   Lesson Plan   *138*
Other Subjects/Classes: I'm Teaching What?!   *139*
   Special Education   *140*
   History   *141*
   Geography   *141*
   Social Studies   *141*
   English as a Second Language   *141*
   Computers   *141*
   Library   *142*
   Language, Math, Science   *142*

Chapter 8: On the Way to the Job You Want   *145*

When No Schools are Calling   *145*
One Day Turns into Two…   *146*
Covering a Maternity/Sick Leave   *147*
How to Get a Permanent Job by Making Everyone Happy   *149*
   Make the Students Happy   *149*
   Make the Absent Teacher Happy   *149*
   Make the Other Teachers Happy   *150*
   Make the Vice-Principal and Principal Happy   *150*
   Make the School Secretaries Happy   *150*
   Make Yourself Happy   *151*
Is This What My Career Is Supposed to Look Like?   *151*
Advantages to Substitute Teaching   *152*
   No Paperwork   *152*
   Flexibility   *152*
   Exploration   *153*
   The Hours   *153*
   The Pay   *153*
   Easy Days   *153*

Acknowledgments   *155*
Recommended Resources   *156*
Index   *157*

Introduction

Substitute teaching can be a great job where both you and the students really enjoy the day and look forward to the next time you can be together. Of course, some days it seems like you are simply surviving. Or barely surviving (I think I need some chocolate!). This can be especially true when you first start substitute teaching, because it is very different from being a permanent teacher. You need to be excellent at classroom management, without the benefit of having an ongoing relationship with the students and without the benefit of being able to enforce consequences. Students know you will not be marking their work or writing their report cards, calling their parents, or—heaven forbid—moving their desks away from their friends!

Despite these difficulties, you do not have to simply survive the days. You can make it fun—get silly or get the kids laughing. They also will give you plenty of stories to keep you and your friends amused and entertained! Students can have fun while they learn. You can have a fulfilling career. Your attitude and your approach make all the difference. It takes practice and you will get better at it as you work on it. But you can have really successful days from the moment you decide to have fun.

Substitute teaching can be simple. You don't have to carry around a big bag of supplies, or have half a dozen premade lesson plans, or take copious amounts of notes. It doesn't have to be difficult or take up a lot of your time before or after school. A few items in your bag and an emergency plan for when the teacher is unable to leave a day plan is all you need. This is one of the great things about substitute teaching—it is neither as complicated nor as much work as a permanent teaching job. It is pretty simple: you go to school about 15 minutes before it starts and leave about 15 minutes after it ends. No fuss, no muss, no planning, no meetings, no headaches because you're in the room beside instrumental music all year!

Admittedly, there are things that are difficult in substitute teaching. But these things can be made simple. Having strategies in place to handle students who won't do their work or who won't listen makes things a lot easier.

You got into teaching because you wanted to make a difference in kids' lives, right? You wanted to make a difference in the world. You wanted to help kids know who they are and who they want to be. You wanted to encourage them to be their best and help them learn and overcome difficulties. And just maybe you wanted to be like that teacher who really affected your life.

This can seem difficult when you see different students every day. But you can still make a difference—a big difference—in students' lives. In the past, students have seen bad substitute teachers. How do you think we got the reputation we have? Those teachers yelled—a lot—and didn't care about the students. Students can tell if someone cares about them or not. When you go in and you actually care, it makes a difference. You have a whole day to influence the students. It is stressful for students to have a substitute teacher, and you can make their day better by being a great one—or just one who doesn't completely suck! When you have fun and help students learn, it makes a huge difference in their day. You never know—something you say to encourage them might be the thing they needed that day, or that year. It might be the thing they will remember years from now as a turning point in their lives. You just don't know what effect you have.

This book answers the questions: How do I teach students and enjoy it? (Isn't that what we all want? Besides winning the lottery, I mean.) How do I deal with typical problems; e.g., when all 20 Grade 1 students need the bathroom at the same time? What do I need to take with me in my bag and in my attitude? What should I expect—the good, the bad. and the ugly—and what should I do about it?

Just in case you were trained in primary grades and you are substituting for a Grade 8 teacher (or vice-versa), there are tips on teaching students from Kindergarten to Grade 8, including what the average student is like physically, socially, and academically. Also included are complete day plans in case the teacher was called away on an emergency, along with reproducible pages and extra activities. If you find you are teaching one subject for all or part of a day (e.g., Music or Physical Education), there are lesson plans that can be used with all grades for a variety of subjects.

And finally, there is help with ideas about how to have the job you want—whether that's being a career substitute teacher or a permanent teacher—or simply to enjoy the job you have. And how to do that before going broke.

Whether you are a new graduate and want all the help you can get, a retired teacher making the transition from having your own classroom to teaching in a different classroom every day, a career substitute teacher looking to steal some good ideas, or a permanent teacher looking for emergency lesson plans to leave in case you are ever called away without time to plan for the substitute, this book offers help. And (hopefully) a few laughs to go with it.

1

Toolkit for Substitute Teaching

Robin Williams, as Peter Pan in the movie *Hook*, uses "Chemistry Substitute Teacher" as an insult. This is funny because, in part, it is true! In the past, substitute teachers have had a bad reputation; however, our generation of substitute teachers is able to change this. By being excellent substitute teachers, by having a positive and creative attitude, and by the way we talk about our profession, we can change the perception of the profession of substitute teaching. It is time!

First, we need to be excellent. We need to do our job so that students enjoy their day and learn. Next, we need to talk about our profession with respect, so that others do too. We need to let people know that we have an excellent profession in which we get to make a difference in the lives of many children, helping them when their teacher is away. It's time to give ourselves the respect we deserve and to expect it from others. It's time to change the cultural norm around the noble profession of substitute teaching.

The First Ten Minutes: Getting Their Attention

Substitute teaching is fun. At least, it can be fun! It can also be the absolute worst job ever. Of course, you want to make it as much fun as possible. How do you do that? It's all about the first ten minutes. The first ten minutes pretty much sets the tone for the rest of the class or the rest of the day. It's important to get the kids on your side right away. Then, the rest of the day is a lot easier and more enjoyable.

You want to build a good relationship with the students as fast as possible. This is what they respond to—seeing you as a real person and being treated like real people. When you tell them about yourself, when you tell a good story, it helps build that relationship. When you start with a great first ten minutes, you are quickly building a good relationship so that they will want to listen to you. They will want to do what you ask. By handing out incentives and telling gross stories, you get the students on your side. Many substitute teachers yell in the first ten minutes of the day. This sets an adversarial tone—which the students love to take advantage of. You know, it's fun to try to get the substitute teacher mad enough not to come back! This is what you should try to avoid.

We've all had days of substitute teaching where the kids didn't tell us their own names, sat in someone else's seat, changed the time on the clock, set off a stink

The way you deal with chatty (or rebellious) students is another make or break point; see page 16.

Of course, you can have a great first ten minutes and then have the tone change part way through the day. Students are often more difficult to handle in the afternoon, after going to the store and buying sugar for lunch.

bomb in the class, wouldn't listen at all, and in general were plain bad. (Oh, sorry. The kids were not bad; their behavior was bad. I am, of course, not making a moral judgment about the students themselves.) You know, the days when you really have to control yourself to keep from just losing it. Instead, I do something to get them on my side, like tell a ghost story or a gross fact. I find the students quiet down and are more likely to work quietly after I'm done, especially if I say I will tell another one when everyone finishes their work!

When students first enter the classroom, I give incentives to the first couple of students who sit down quietly. I loudly announce I have given an incentive to these students because they sat down quickly and quietly and soon all students are sitting down quietly.

This is when I give my speech. I introduce myself. I point out my name written on the board to avoid the question, "What is your name again?" for the one-hundredth time that day (not that this always works) and tell them I am an excellent substitute teacher. I tell students that I give out incentives, tell gross, scary, and funny stories, and that I rarely raise my voice. Then I ask if they want to hear a gross fact.

> Bears don't go to the bathroom during the winter. They sleep, right? Actually, they do go to the bathroom during the winter. But the poop just stays inside them and forms a kind of plug inside their bottoms called a fecal plug! That's why they're so angry in the spring—not only are they hungry, but also a bit constipated. That's not the gross fact though. The gross fact is that bear cubs (baby bears) also go to the bathroom during the winter. However, they don't go on the cave floor because it would get dirty and they could get sick. Does anyone have a guess what happens to the bear cubs' poop?

I allow students to guess the answer, giving hints along the way. I give an incentive (e.g., a sticker or candy) to the student who answers correctly.

> Answer: The mother bear licks it off them and eats it.

This gross fact is one of the ways I get students quiet, listening to me, and on my side.

Bag of Tools for Keeping Their Attention (and Staying Sane)

Humor can be there in your bag of tools. But even if you don't really have a sense of humor (of course, everyone thinks they have a sense of humor, so I'm sure you do too) you can still get the kids to like you.

Every substitute teacher needs a bag of tools. The more tools you have, the better chance you have of having fun and getting work done, no matter how challenging the students are. My favorite tools include incentives; gross, funny, and scary stories; and magic tricks. When one tool doesn't work, you just pull out another one. I save the hammer over the head for the end, after I threaten no more incentives for the day (this almost always works).

Incentives/Rewards

Edible

You might not want to, or may not be allowed to, hand out candy. There are other effective tools and incentives you can use—this is just the most fun one! You know, children's love is for sale. You can buy it with sugar. You can be a pretty bad substitute teacher and, if you give them candy, they will love you.

When handing out candy, first and foremost, you need to make sure you buy candy that is peanut-free. This means making sure it doesn't have *May have come into contact with nuts or nut products* or *May contain traces of nuts* on the package. I also recommend gelatin-free candy: gelatin is a meat byproduct, so children who can't eat meat (or pork) for any reason can't eat candy with gelatin.

I often tell the students that they are allowed to eat the candy right away (some of them are going to try to eat it anyway). I make sure to tell them that the first time I see a candy wrapper on the floor I will stop handing out candy. Then when I do see a wrapper on the floor, I say, "I'm sure I don't see a wrapper on the floor because then I wouldn't be handing out any more candy." I keep going on and on about it until someone picks it up.

I do *not* give out candy to every kid—except maybe in Kindergarten, but I find in Kindergarten it is not needed. I give candy only to those who do what they are asked to do. Sometimes I hand out only two candies a day, or none; sometimes ten candies a class. I make sure the kids know that I am not going to be "fair" and hand one out to everyone. Why would they do what I want if they're going to get one anyway? I tell them, "You can get two or three candies if you answer the questions, do your work, etc." After a short while, the kids know that the first one sitting or finished gets a candy, so they sit quickly and get their work done quickly. I also sometimes give out candy if I see a student taking positive initiative; e.g., cleaning up without prompting or helping someone without being asked.

Non-Edible

In primary classes you can give out stickers instead of candy. This is particularly good for children with ADHD, as sugar does not usually help them focus! In junior and intermediate classes, I sometimes give out sticky notes with *Get out of trouble free* written on them. Then, if that student gets in trouble, they can give me their sticky and they are not in trouble anymore. Of course, I make sure they understand that the sticky note works only with me and not with other teachers. Stickers, pencils, and temporary tattoos also work for little kids. Fake teeth, eyes, fake spiders, fake poo, or anything gross works for older kids; these are a bit more expensive, so you have to make qualifying for them more difficult so you hand out fewer.

Free Time

Not all students want a sticker or a *get out of trouble free* card. But all students want free time! This is probably the most commonly used incentive among substitute teachers. Many teachers put a number on the board—for example, 10—and tell students that is how many minutes of free time they have at the end of the period. If students are noisy, the number is dropped to 9. If students are quiet, the number can be raised to 11. You need to have a stop watch to make sure you give them the exact number of minutes you said you would or it won't work the next time you see that class.

I buy candy at the discount store and I only buy the packages that cost a dollar for about thirty candies. It's definitely worth the money. I also make sure I only buy candies I don't like so that I don't eat them.

You can be more vague if you want more flexibility, telling students when they are chatty that perhaps they will not get free time at the end of the period. I find that it is best to try to give free time at the end of each period instead of just at the end of the day. The end of the day sometimes seems just too far away to worry about!

Games

Students love games. Intermediate students sometimes try to act too cool to like games but, when you find a good game, these students are the most competitive of all! If you have already given free time once or twice, you can try using the incentive of a game. Even classic games like hot potato and charades can be really exciting for primary and junior students. There is an Internet full of games, not to mention numerous books. However, I find the best way to find a good game is to ask another teacher.

Magic

Magic tricks are a great tool. I highly recommend learning a handful of them and practicing. All kids like candies and all kids like magic. Here are a couple of tricks I use; you can look up the rest online.

Where's the Coin

This is a sleight-of-hand trick that can be perfected with a bit of practice. The goal is to make it look like the coin is in one hand when it is actually in the other.
- Hold a small coin (a penny or dime) between your thumb and index finger so the audience can see the picture on the coin, with your palm facing up.
- Bring your other hand in front of the coin as though to take it from the first hand into the second. But instead of taking the coin, drop it from your fingers to the palm of the hand the coin is already in (see diagram in margin). The audience will not see the coin drop because your other hand is blocking their view.
- Pretend to take the coin with the second hand.
- Close both palms and turn your hands over and ask students to guess where the coin is.

Disappearing Coin

A second—and better—trick is making the coin disappear. This trick is a huge favorite with kids!
- Put one hand up to your ear; with the other hand, rub a coin against your elbow (see diagram in margin).
- Drop the coin and pick it up with the hand that was up against your ear. Transfer it to the other hand and continue rubbing it on your elbow with one hand against your ear.
- Drop it again; pick it up and continue rubbing it on your elbow.
- Drop it a third time; this time, only pretend to transfer the coin from one hand to the other. Pretend to rub the coin on your elbow. As you put the hand with the coin in it to your ear, place the coin in your ear.
- Show students both empty hands. Have them guess where the coin is and then show them it's in your ear.

For a video on how to do the Where's the Coin trick, check out amandayuill.com

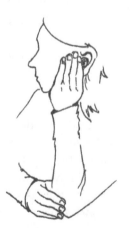

For a video on how to do the Disappearing Coin trick, check out amandayuill.com

12

For a video on how to do the How to Freak Out Your Mom trick, check out amandayuill.com

How to Freak Out Your Mom

I tell students I'm going to show them a way to freak out their mom!
- Hold up one hand.
- With all the other fingers up, let the ring finger fall down. Push it back a bit.
- Flick the end of your ring finger up and down (see diagram in margin). Do this very fast and it looks kind of cool!
- Tell the kids to do it and tell their moms they broke their finger in class today.

Jokes (in Case You're Not Funny)

Here's a knock-knock joke that kills in primary grades.

> A: Knock, knock.
> B: Who's there?
> A: Banana.
> B: Banana who?
> A: Knock, knock.
> B: Who's there?
> A: Banana.
> B: Banana who?
> A: Knock, knock.
> B: Who's there?
> A: Orange.
> B: Orange who?
> A: Orange you glad I didn't say banana again?

Gross Facts

You can get these gross facts from the Internet or from books, such as the Uncle John Bathroom Reader series.
- A mother tiger shark has lots of babies in her womb but only one is born because the strongest baby shark eats the rest in her womb.
- In South America they found a cave with piles of cockroaches. The cockroaches never leave the cave. They eat bat feces.
- A hippo mom feeds her baby milk, but it is not white. It is pink.

Scary Stories that Won't Cause Nightmares

Students love ghost stories. I try to tell ones that are more freaky or funny than scary, as some students do get bad dreams from scary stories. Here's my favorite:

> My dad moved to Toronto about fifty years ago. He used to work for the Toronto Transit Commission, fixing buses. He worked night shift from 11 p.m. to 6 a.m. One night, his boss let him go early at 4 a.m. He decided to walk home instead of taking the bus so he could get to know Toronto a bit better. Unfortunately, after he started walking, it started getting foggy and he lost his way.
>
> He stopped at a donut store for a coffee and a donut and spoke with the man behind the counter, who turned out to be the owner of the store. My dad told the owner that he had lost his way and mentioned where he lived. The owner didn't know where it was, but the customer sitting next to my

dad did. He said he was going to take the streetcar home and that my dad's apartment was on the way. He'd tell my dad where to get off the streetcar to get home. They finished eating and headed out for the streetcar. However, as my dad was walking towards the streetcar, he got a strange feeling that he didn't want to take the streetcar. He asked the man if he could get home by following the streetcar tracks. The man told him to turn right when he got to McDonalds and his apartment building would be right there. My dad thanked the man, who got on the streetcar and waved good-bye.

My dad followed the streetcar tracks and turned right at McDonalds. However, his apartment building wasn't there—the man had given him wrong directions. He did recognize the area, so he decided to walk around a bit until he found his apartment. It took him an hour and he got home at 6 a.m. He slept until noon and got up and read the newspaper. On the front was a picture of the man who gave him the wrong directions. It said he had been missing for three days. My dad thought about calling the police to tell them he'd seen that man the night before, but he wasn't sure it was the same man. He decided to go back to the donut store to ask the owner if he also thought it was the same person. If the owner agreed that it was the same person, my dad would call the police.

My dad found McDonalds and headed up the same street. He found the donut store but it was all boarded up!! He went next door to the fish-and-chips shop and asked the girl behind the counter why they had boarded up the store that morning. The lady told him that there had been a fire three days before. The owner had died in the fire, and they had boarded up the store that very day. My dad was pretty freaked out, so he asked her what time the next streetcar came so he could get home. The lady asked him what he was talking about—there was no streetcar on that street! Sure enough, he went outside and there were no streetcar tracks on that road.

Funny Stories

It's best if you use funny stories from your own life, but any funny story will do. Here's one of mine:

When I first moved to Japan to teach English, I didn't know any Japanese so I would study new words every day. One day I studied adjectives. That night I was on the bus, sitting near the back and reading a book. They turned off all the lights at the back of the bus but left on the lights at the front. I wanted to move forward so I could keep reading and I also wanted to let the lady sitting beside me know why I was moving. I had learned the word for "dark" that day so I could say to her, "It's dark, isn't it?" I said this to her and moved forward. The next day as I was reading over my words, I realized I'd used the wrong adjective. I hadn't said to her, "It's dark, isn't it?" I had said, "You're dirty, aren't you?"

I also called my boss "Mr. Shrimp" by mistake. He was shorter than me.

All About You

The students want to know about you. Are you married? Do you have kids? Have you travelled? Do you have hobbies? Anything you tell them, they will be interested, especially if you have some funny stories or interesting anecdotes (and especially if it means they aren't doing work during the time you're talking about yourself).

Classroom Management, NOT Babysitting

At least 80 per cent of substitute teaching is behavior management, which is why substitute teachers sometimes have the reputation of being babysitters. But this is not true, and anyone who has tried substitute teaching knows it. Behavior management is one of the biggest and most challenging parts of the job, so here are a few tips.

Attendance

It is a mistake to try to take attendance right away. Students in Grade 4 and higher will switch names and desks. I let them sit wherever they want and tell them that if they get in trouble, I'll move them. I don't say, "Hey, everyone, sit where you want"—but when the tattletale tells me someone's not sitting where he or she is supposed to, I don't make them move. Of course, if someone wants to sit in their own desk and someone else is sitting there, I make that person move. All this to say, the students will definitely try to give you the wrong name. Which is why I tell jokes and gross stories and hand out candies first. Students are less likely to lie to someone who has made them laugh and given them candy.

If I still think many of them will give me the wrong names, I give the task of taking attendance to the quiet kid in the front row. If I'm going to be at that school for a few days, I memorize the students' names. Whatever the student tells me their name is, that's what I call them (within reason, of course; I don't call anyone Fartman, for example). But I review the names every so often. When I'm near the quiet girl in the front row, I pretend to forget some of the names; i.e., the names of the students I think gave me the wrong names. I ask the quiet kid, "What is that student's name again?" The kid tells me the right one. When I start calling the students by their actual names, they usually just answer back, forgetting they told me another name.

Students Who Make You Earn Your Pay

It's useful to find out who usually gives the substitute teacher problems. When the secretary or vice-principal is showing me the way to the classroom, I sometimes ask if there are any students I should be aware of. Actually, I usually find out by asking the students in class, "Whose name should I know in this class?" They all point to the same one or two students—who are usually pointing to themselves! Start out by asking these students to help; this can prevent a lot of unwanted behavior. Ask them to take the attendance to the office, to tell you where certain supplies are, or to be first in line to lead you to the library.

If a "problem student" gets out of control during the day, I ask him/her to take a note to the office that says, *Please look at this and say "Thank you" and send this student back; this student just needed a walk.* I will sometimes ask a student to get a drink of water and go to the bathroom and then come back. If the student tells me he/she doesn't need a drink of water or to go to the bathroom, I tell the student that this is his/her chance to have a bit of a break and then to come back and change how they are behaving.

Please, Stop Talking!

I have seen substitute teachers use a whistle to get kids to stop talking. Or you could always try yelling, clapping hands, turning lights off and on, and threatening to call the office. None of these work very well if overused. Of course, handing out incentives or candy is my favorite way of getting students to be quiet. But when students are already strung out on sugar overload after lunch, there are other ways to do it.

Humor is the best (i.e., most fun) way to get quiet. When you call for quiet, most of the students will eventually quiet down (give them thirty seconds to one minute). There will be only a few students who are still talking. If it is a junior or intermediate class, I usually say, "I'm totally cool and a great teacher and I look great today, so of course you want to spend more time with me. I know you want to spend more time with me after school/during recess today, but you don't have to talk to do it. You can just say, 'Ms. Yuill, I really want to spend time with you at recess/after school', and I'll let you." This usually gets them laughing and stops everybody but *the one* from talking.

You know *the one*: the class clown who is out to get a reaction from you, preferably that you get angry and give the student the power. When a kid is talking and his/her back is to me, I stand right behind that student, put my face close to the back of his/her head, smile a cheesy smile, and say nothing. The other kids start to laugh and so the talker turns around to find my face is really close—the kid jumps back, which makes everyone laugh more. *The one* will usually laugh and pay attention for all of 20 seconds before talking again. At which point, I just sit on that student's desk to continue teaching.

If *the one* is facing me, I ask, "What are you doing? Because I can totally see you talking." I explain:

> First, you're supposed to look around to see if the teacher is looking and, if she isn't, you can talk. But I was totally looking, so what are you doing? And it's no good to have your hand up to your mouth to whisper to the person beside you, because I can still totally tell you're talking. If you don't want me to know, you have to wait until I'm not looking and then don't use your hand—it's a total giveaway.

There's No Playing Tag Inside

Touching is sometimes a problem. Some students seem to get a kick out of touching each other in not-nice ways. This can lead to two kids running around the classroom—and that's guaranteed to be when the vice-principal looks in the classroom window! To stop this, I tell students that there is no hugging in class and that if they want to hug, they can do it at recess. This gets a laugh and the kids stop chasing each other.

Sometimes when students are chasing each other around the classroom, it is a cue that they need a movement break. You can see when a class, especially a primary class, is getting antsy, so I have students stand up and do 5 jumping jacks, 5 hops on one foot, 5 hops on the other foot, 5 spins, 5 sit-ups, 5 seconds running on the spot, etc.—anything to get them moving a bit. After doing this for up to five minutes, I have students sit down and then I continue with my lesson. This often helps students focus more easily and get more work done with less fooling around.

> ### Faking It
>
> When the students are a really hard bunch, I tell them that the work has to be done in class or at home, but I don't care where; it just has to be done for their teacher by the next day. As long as they look like they are working, I'm fine with that. They have to have something open on their desk and a pen or pencil in their hand. The noise level has to be not too bad. Otherwise, they can do what they want—reading, drawing, chatting quietly with friends—within reason. I find it amazing how many students actually do their work when I give this option. It also means that when the vice-principal peeks through the window, the students will look like they are doing work!

Getting Students to Do Their Work

Why, oh why won't they do their work? It's school—they know they come here to learn. But all they're doing is chatting and fooling around! When a class sits and does their work without any protests, I always write a note to the teacher telling them how well-behaved the class is! On most days, however, I use anything from the bag of tools—everything from the bag of tools (see page 10)! If these fail to work, I turn the work into a game or a competition. I tell them it is a contest to see which group/gender/grade finishes first.

I also let students know I will be collecting the work. Sometimes they think they can take work home and "lose" it to get out of doing it. I also let them know that we will be taking it up at the end of the period. When students know there is an end in sight, it helps them focus. So I tell them how much time they have left and what they should have already accomplished: e.g., "You should have your name and date written by now" or "There are ten minutes left. You should have the first side of the paper finished by now." If worse comes to worst, I tell them that the principal may be walking through the halls looking into classrooms that day and I want them to be doing work when this happens. This is true, as principals are often in the halls and do sometimes look into classrooms!

The Afternoon

Everything was fine in the morning. Then, there was an assembly first thing in the afternoon. It was too long. Recess was delayed and then shortened. The kids came back *crazy*. Afternoons are often more difficult than mornings. This is where I use a lot of the tools I have.

- Students often need to move around, so I tell them if they finish their work early, we can have DPA (Daily Physical Activity)—outside, if the weather is nice.
- Sometimes we have a quick movement break even if it's just after lunch or recess.
- I find that if I tell a story or two—especially a story that has a serious or scary ending, like a ghost story—I can keep students quieter. Remember: not too scary, because some students get nightmares…
- It's a good idea to have the students put their heads down on their desks and listen to quiet music for a couple of minutes.

Sometimes there is a run on the bathroom—like they're handing out gold toilet paper or something. When students keep asking if they can go to the bathroom—or to prevent a run on the can—I ask if they can wait two to three minutes and then ask me again. Often they forget. The ones who really do have to go ask again and I let them go.

- If students have work to do, I often don't let them talk at all (or whisper if they need help), to help keep them calm.
- I walk around more during the afternoon, as it helps students to be quieter when there is a teacher near—I'm kind of like a Star Trek dampening field.

Recess Problems—Not Your Problem

Students often come back from recess with problems with each other: "Neela hit me" or "David took my ball." This can be annoying. Very, very annoying. Usually I ask if the student has told the person to stop it and to apologize. If they haven't, I tell them to do that first and if the other person doesn't apologize, to tell a teacher tomorrow! If they have, I ask if the student told a teacher on yard duty. If yes, I tell the student to talk about it with that teacher after school.

If none of this works, I ask if the problem happens often. If yes, I tell the student to talk about it with the regular teacher when he/she gets back. If the problem remains unresolved, I ask the students to stay after school and tell me about it and I'll try to fix it as best I can. They rarely stay.

Of course, all of this is to say I try my hardest not to deal with recess problems. If I must, I try to do it quickly. Of course, if there's blood or a bump, I find out what happened.

To Call or Not to Call—the Office

I rarely send kids to the office; however, there are times when it is not only appropriate but also wise. One time, a student told me that she was going to hit me. She went to the office. All this because I told her she had to sit in a seat like everyone else. Most schools have a code of behavior that lists offences for which students are sent to the office. These include threatening a teacher or a student, swearing at a teacher, physically hitting/kicking a teacher or student, having a weapon, and making racist comments. I would add nudity (yes, it happens). I try not to be too strict when it comes to discipline, preferring the use of humor to a raised voice, and the carrot to the stick. But there is a place for strict discipline. Here are some ideas of what to do besides using a raised voice:
- Withdrawal of Privileges: Make the student ineligible to win incentives for the next period or have him/her sit out during free time or a game.
- Isolation: Place the student alone, away from other students. Send the student to get a drink and go to the bathroom, or stand out in the hall for five minutes. Tell the student this is time for him/her to calm down and to come back ready to behave properly.
- Reporting: Leave a note for the teacher saying how bad that student has been. In fact, just threatening to do this often improves behavior if they have a good teacher; if not, they don't care and the threat is worthless, as is the note.
- Ignoring: Give up. As long as they aren't hurting each other or being vandals, sometimes you're just not paid enough and it isn't worth the trouble. You can always choose not to go back to that school. There are some advantages to substitute teaching, after all.

When you have tried a variety of strategies and there is still a student who is being very disruptive and rude, and who is leading others to do the same, it is okay to send that student to the office. You don't have to feel bad or like you're a failure. We all need help sometimes. It can be a wise choice to send a student to the office, as the rest of the class will often settle down and do their work.

A Perspective to Help You Not Be Angry

Some students are unable to control their behavior. This is helpful to know, as it might change how you handle a situation. If you think a student is able to stop moving around, you will be angry when he/she doesn't; however, if you believe a student is unable to help him/herself, you will treat that student very differently. There are often distracting students in class. Often these kids have ADHD and are unable to sit still. When they get very distracting, I send them to get a drink, to use the bathroom, or on a made-up errand. Giving an overactive student a job is also a good idea; e.g., there are art supplies, and they are not usually neat. In the case of uber-organized teachers whose classes are quiet and get their work done and who leave three pages of notes for substitute teachers, DO NOT let the kids with ADHD touch the art supplies! That teacher will never ask you back!

Finding Your Own Style

It's important to find your own style. In this chapter, I've shared my style and a few of my tricks with you. As you teach, you will develop your own style. You may be more laid-back and allow students to chat more. You may be stricter and require students to work quietly. It's important to try out many different things and see what works for you and what doesn't. Please don't tell gross facts if it makes you feel sick. Please don't tell ghost stories if you get nightmares. Unlike me, you may be able to make your ears wiggle or stick out your tongue and touch your nose. Personalize it!

What to Take With You

In a world without gravity, you could take a suitcase full of materials. However, after a week of lugging it all around, most of us come to realize we don't have superstrength. So, here's what you really need:

- Pencil: Some teachers lock pencils in their desks, leaving you to borrow from a student to do attendance.
- Whistle: Gym and yard duty are much easier with it.
- Incentives/Rewards: These work well for everyone from Kindergarten to Grade 8! Discount-store candy is great: even Grade 8 kids quiet down if you give them one, although they could just go buy it with their allowance money after school! Stickers and temporary tattoos are also favorites.
- This book: or have at least some pages copied in case there are no day plans.

Yard/Recess Duty

Teachers try to take the day off when they have yard duty, because who wants to do yard duty? So you will likely do yard duty a few times every week. Because of this, it's really important to wear shoes you can stand in for fifteen minutes. You'd be surprised what people wear. Also, in the winter you need to wear clothing warm enough for outdoors. I know, I know, I sound like your mother. But just remember I said so when you're outside shivering away! I take an umbrella with me because some schools still have outdoor recess when there is a "Scottish mist" (thanks, Ms. Poole), or light rain. Also, I get sunburned easily so I use it on sunny days too.

Pembroke Publishers ©2016 *Substitute Teaching?* by Amanda Yuill ISBN 978-1-55138-312-5

2

A Typical Day Substitute Teaching: An Oxymoron

Before Students Arrive

Finding the School

You are going to a new school and the map says it should be right where you are, but it is not. You are not lost—you know where you are. Clearly, the school is lost. Then, you find the school—but only the back of the schoolyard. Where is the entrance? Okay, you found the entrance after walking three-quarters of the way around the school. And the door is locked—which door is open? Oh, the first one you tried has a doorbell you're supposed to ring.

Be sure to leave the house early the first time you are going to a new school. You don't want to be late. Actually, I don't really know about you; *I* don't want to be late. It is really helpful to get to the school 15 minutes early so you can get ready for the day. This might include reading the lesson plans, finding the textbooks, feeding the class gerbil, or any other number of tasks.

Finding the Classroom

Next, you find your way to the office by asking directions or by following signs—or miraculously it is right inside the door you entered! At the office, the secretary/administrator/person behind the desk has you sign in and then shows you to your room, pointing out the staff bathrooms and staffroom on the way. She (or he) hands you the day plans or tells you they are on the teacher's desk; gives you helpful hints about the class and school. Or she (or he) mumbles a room number and points vaguely in some direction, at which point you ask politely where the staff bathroom is—the rest you can find out later.

Being Flexible

But I don't speak French and I can't sing. I'm pretty sure I agreed to a Grade 2 class, not French Immersion Music! It is common to reach a school and find out that the job accepted is not the job they want you to do. Part way through the day, the teaching assignment can change: in the morning you were going to be teaching Grade 5 all day; at lunch they ask if you can teach ESL. As much as possible, I agree to change and teach whatever it is they want me to teach.

To this end, it is always good to wear comfortable shoes, or at least have a pair with you, because teaching gym all day is not out of the question. The only time I really hesitate is when they want me to go on a field trip and I am not wearing appropriate clothing. This can be a safety issue (if I'm wearing my cute heels and they are going on a hike) or a health issue (if I'm wearing my cool fall leather jacket and it is snowing), so I simply explain why I'm hesitating and make clear that I would be willing to do anything else. Flexibility is a very highly valued quality in a substitute teacher.

It is annoying, inconvenient, and just not-so-good to have to change teaching assignments last minute. But when you do, principals, vice-principals, and office administrators take notice. They call you back. I highly recommend finding a way to become okay with this adaptability if you are not naturally flexible (yes, I'm speaking to you other type-A personalities out there who like to plan and prepare ahead of time). It might help even just to know that this might happen so you can be mentally prepared. Some schools tend to do this more than others, so if it really bothers you, you can always try to work at schools where this does not happen so much.

Finding the Day Plans—Or Not

First thing is to find the day plans, if the office did not have them. They are usually on the teacher's desk, although sometimes they are in that teacher's box in the staff room or office, along with the attendance. Many teachers leave excellent, detailed day plans and lesson plans, along with all necessary materials, placed neatly on the desk. They leave notes about classroom routines; e.g., which door to pick up the students and where they eat lunch. Teachers often leave helpful notes about how to help certain students stay seated and learn well that day, and which students will answer honestly if you need help.

Once you find the day plans, it's good to go over them to make sure you understand them; i.e., you can read the teacher's writing. It's also good to make sure you have all the materials you need. Sometimes the teacher says the lesson is on page 351 but there are only 267 pages in the book. Oh, wait, this is the Grade 1 math book, not the Grade 2 math book—or is this the science book? I try to get all of the materials I need for each lesson organized so I can quickly pick them up and start the lesson when it's time.

If the day plans are not on the desk or in the teacher's box, ask at the office. If a teacher doesn't know until the last moment that he or she won't be in that day, the day plans might be e-mailed to another teacher or to the office. It sometimes takes until 15 or 20 minutes after the school day has started for the office to find the plans; if this is the case, you can ask another teacher or the students what they usually do for the first period. Or you can use the time to tell the students about yourself and find out about them. Or you can have them read quietly.

If the teacher was called away on an emergency, often another teacher will know what the class is learning and will be able to give you materials and ideas for the day. Some schools have each teacher prepare an emergency folder of materials for just this kind of situation. Hopefully, you can find someone who knows where it is.

If there is absolutely nothing, it's a good thing you have a plan! This is where really good substitute teachers step up to the plate. Because you got to the school early, you still have time to photocopy or print off the pages from this book (see chapters 3 to 6). Principals and vice-principals really appreciate it when you have enough initiative to handle this situation.

If there isn't time to prepare before classes begin, you can do introduction activities, quiet reading, and a creative writing activity until first recess, then you can photocopy or print pages from this book to use.

Last-Minute Preparation

Write your name on the blackboard.

Ask yourself: *Do I have the attendance? Do I have my self-introduction materials ready: a coin for a magic trick or stickers for children who sit down quietly? Where was the teacher bathroom again? Did I check the mirror?* Sometimes I look at myself at lunch and think, "Oh, no, is that how I looked all morning? Why didn't I check the mirror sooner?"

If you finish your preparations early, it is always good to say hello to the teachers in the hallway or in the classroom beside you. They will often have tips that will help you have success with the class you are teaching that day. It's also a good way to become better known in that school—sometimes teachers may ask you if you are available for a day in the future when they need a substitute teacher!

With Students

Enter the Students

If you are teaching Kindergarten to Grade 6, you will likely go to a door to pick up the students up from outside and lead them to the classroom. If you are teaching Grades 7 or 8, the students will probably enter and go to their lockers themselves before coming to the classroom. Often there is five to ten minutes between the time the students enter the school and the national anthem. It is best to try to have all students sitting quietly at their desks by then. This can be difficult in winter with primary students, as they have many layers to take off and sometimes still have difficulty with zippers, buttons, and laces. (This unfortunately applies to some intermediate students as well… No finger-pointing at your friends, now!)

Self-Introduction and Attendance

Although the attendance usually needs to get to the office within ten minutes of the national anthem, I try to do a couple of self-introduction activities first. It makes attendance go easier.

Classroom Routines

All teachers have their own routines set up to help things flow easily. Students will want things to stay as close as possible to their regular routine. This is especially true for younger students. Older ones are much more able to go with the flow, roll with the punches, and perform other impressive idioms. Students will all eagerly tell you the "right" way to do it, as you are clearly doing it the "wrong" way. As much as possible, I try to keep to the daily routines as the teacher has left in her day plans and as students tell me when I make mistakes. When this comes up, I let the students know that I will do some things differently from their teacher. Hopefully they will like these changes—like offering incentives; however, I tell them that I will be doing some things differently and that's just how it's going to be.

Doing the Work the Teacher Left

If students say that they have already done the lesson and most of them can show me the work in their books, and if it is math or science or something where they are following a textbook, I sometimes simply move on to the next lesson in the book. But usually I just have students do a review lesson.

As much as possible, do the work the teacher left, even if it seems trivial or appears to be too difficult. Trusting the teacher is what sets you apart as an excellent substitute teacher. It is amazing how often a substitute teacher will think the lesson is too hard or too easy (for them as often as for the students) and so will do something else. This can really throw a wrench into the teacher's plans and schedule. A good substitute does what is left, no matter what students say—"Oh, we already did this" or "This is too easy/difficult" or "I'm not doing this" or "If we give you our lunch, will you just say we did it?" Just tell students that their teacher knew they had already done this lesson and she left it for review, so they should all get perfect on it.

Sometimes students will tell me that they don't do language/math/science with the rest of the class, that they do other work the teacher did not mention or did not leave. In this case, I ask students to do their best with what the teacher left. I try to help them get started and ask them to do what they can. I suggest modifications or allow the students to work with a partner if they say they can work quietly (and I believe them).

So you know you are going to do the work the teacher left. How are you going to do it? Sometimes the teacher leaves a detailed lesson to teach, sometimes just handouts or a page number in a textbook. Either way, I try to start the lesson with some fun. I think of a game or a story that is relevant to the lesson, or at least to the subject. If I can't think of anything, I give the instructions really quickly and ask students if they understood and can remember them all. Then I give the instructions slowly. If the instructions are written, I read them out making obvious (and hopefully funny) mistakes so that students correct me.

After I start with a bit of fun, I try to do a very short lesson or introduction. Then I ask students to start working, providing incentives such as promises of free time or money. Okay, I don't offer them money, but sometimes I do wish we were allowed to, as I think it would get many more students to finish their work—or at least start their work!! You wouldn't have to offer that much money to the younger students…

Why do teachers never leave enough work? Why? Why? Why? Okay, not never—just almost never. It seems like even though I go through my self-introduction, games, and the lesson, and then let them do their work and then tell some jokes and stories, the students still have two hours at the end of the day! Free time for two hours is wa-a-a-a-ay too long! I might be exaggerating a bit—but not much. It is very common for students to quickly finish all the work the teacher left and to have a lot of time left over. So have a couple of ideas to take up the time.

It's always a good idea to take up the work. Students can write the answers on the board for math or science, or can read their work aloud for language. It is possible to review what they have learned in the unit they are working on or the unit before, or to have a discussion on the topic. Sometimes I have students color a title page for a unit that includes what they have learned that day. Students can share work with a partner or in a small group. Students can present their work at the front of the class. Sometimes I have everyone stand up at their desks and I ask questions based on the lesson they just had. As they give a correct answer, they can sit down. This continues until everyone has answered a question and is sitting down.

Yard/Hall/Lunchroom Duty

It's good to get some fresh air and exercise—that's what I tell myself when I have yard duty eight times in one week. Yard and various other forms of duty are often a part of the day when you substitute teach. The teachers you are replacing will usually write it down, but sometimes they forget and the office will buzz the classroom or staff room to try to find you to let you know that you are on yard duty. Teachers usually cover a specific area of the yard; if it wasn't left in the day plans or it isn't clear, I just ask another teacher on yard duty what area is my responsibility. Then I have to figure out how to pick up the students in my next class and use the bathroom—which I was going to do over recess!

Dismissal

About ten minutes before recess or lunch or the end of the day, I have students pick up garbage, push in chairs, get on their coats, etc. Some classes are used to cleaning up, others not so much. Some classes have a list of class jobs and some students will clean the board or empty the green bin. When they are ready to go and the bell has rung, primary and junior students will need to be walked to the door or to the lunch room. As with Kindergarten students, primary students are dismissed after school only to the adult (or older sibling) who is picking them up. They do not walk home alone, even if their "mom can see them from the window because they live across the street." Intermediate students usually go to their lockers themselves.

Things That Can Trip You Up

Newsflash: Things don't always go as planned when you are a substitute teacher. It's a chance to grow as a person—at least, that's what I tell myself to keep from saying inappropriate words in front of the kids.

- Sometimes the teacher doesn't say in his/her plans that I have to pick up the students from another teacher, so I sit waiting for them. Either the office will buzz me to let me know where I should be or another teacher will bring the students to me. Sometimes that teacher is annoyed because of the missing ten minutes of prep time that day. Even though it's obviously not your fault, that teacher is mad at you. I usually apologize, saying I didn't know, and that's usually that. I don't take it personally.

- This is unfortunate, but happens often enough to mention. Sometimes as a substitute teacher, other teachers and the administration will try to take advantage of you. They ask you to do things that are not your job: to take another class over your prep period; to stay late to do an extra yard duty or bus duty. As far as possible, I try to accommodate them, because it helps them out and they appreciate it. This can lead to more jobs. However, sometimes it bothers me, especially if what they ask goes over my boundaries. In that case, I politely tell them that I am not comfortable doing what they ask.

3

Substitute Teaching Kindergarten

Help! The Kindergarten Kids Are Eating Me!

Kindergarten children often take a long time to put on their coats, boots, etc. Sometimes it's because they need help but sometimes it's because they are chatting instead of getting ready. I often have a race between the boys and the girls to see who can get ready first. Of course, my nephew's Kindergarten teacher used to do this too. One day, my nephew snuck out to where the coats were and hid all of the girls' scarves and hats so that the boys would win the race, as the boys rarely won. He definitely takes after my brother!

What Kindergarten Students Are Like

Physically

Some children are only three years old when they start Kindergarten; that is very little (and cute)! Many Kindergarten children need help with things that involve small motor skills: everything from holding a pencil or a spoon to doing up buttons and zippers. Using scissors and glue is still very difficult for them. Sitting still is also a skill many Kindergarten children have not yet mastered. Ten minutes is the longest you should have them sitting on the carpet listening. Then it is good to get them up and moving, even if it is simply to stretch, shake their wiggles out, and go on to the next activity.

Kindergarten children love to touch everything. They will touch their friends, the wall, the flowers, the papers, the Velcro on their shoes, and anything they can get their hands on. I mean, why wouldn't you touch it if it's right there in front of you? To help them with this, I often have them say this little rhyme with me.

> Open them (children open their hands); shut them (children make a fist);
> open them (children open their hands); shut them (children make a fist).
> Give a little clap (children clap once).
> Open them (children open their hands); shut them (children make a fist);
> open them (children open their hands); shut them (children make a fist).
> Fold them in your lap (children fold their hands in their lap).

Keep your hands and feet to yourself is a very important rule and Kindergarten students will need to be reminded of it often. If you are walking in the hallway with the class to take them to the library or gym, have them put their hands on their heads as you walk through the hall. Some teachers have students put one hand in front of their mouth with one finger up to remind them also to be quiet.

Besides touching everything, some Kindergarten children still put things in their mouths. Lego blocks, pencils, hair, fingers, thumbs, and, really, anything small enough will go into their mouths. It's important to remind children not to put things in their mouths. Some children do this when they are nervous or tired; if a child continues to put things in his or her mouth, you might ask if he/she is tired or worried about something.

And small children do get tired. If children are especially cranky, they might simply need a rest. It might be a good idea to allow a child to sit and read quietly if he or she is tired, especially in the afternoon. If you find many children seem tired, take a ten-minute break and have students sit and listen to quiet music. They can chat quietly with a friend near them or just listen.

Some Kindergarten children are still getting the hang of toilet training—accidents can happen. Parents often put extra clothing in children's backpacks in case of an accident. If there is no extra clothing in the backpack, send the child to the office with a friend to have the office administrator call home; sometimes they have extra clothes in the office for such incidents.

If a child complains he or she is sick, ask the student to use the bathroom and get a drink of water and then to see if he/she feels better. If the child continues to complain and seems to be warm, pale, or in pain, send the child to the office. Otherwise, I ask children to wait a bit and to tell their parents how they feel when they come to pick them up. If a child throws up in class, send the child to the office with a friend once he or she is calm. Call the office and ask them to send a caretaker to clean up the mess. Keep the other children away from the mess and, if you have to, ask them not to laugh or make fun of the child who was sick.

Children start to lose teeth in Kindergarten. It is a serious rite of passage for them. This is a big deal and something to be celebrated. Children who have not yet lost teeth are envious of those who have. If a child loses a tooth, you will need to secure the tooth in a tissue so the child can take it home for the Tooth Fairy. Have the child rinse out his/her mouth, as there may be some blood. Some schools have little resealable plastic bags in the office just for teeth.

Socially

Someone will probably cry during the day. Hopefully, it won't be you! Kindergarten children cry easily, especially at the beginning of the year. They cry when their parents leave, when they fall, when a friend hurts their feelings, when they get frustrated, when they get tired, or for reasons that are unclear. When a child cries, it is a good idea to find out why and fix the problem if possible, or to try to console or distract them so that they feel better. Sometimes a child just needs to cry for a while and it is okay for them to sit and cry for a few minutes (especially if they are crying because you are enforcing a consequence).

In Kindergarten, there is often a child who refuses to be part of the group. Of course, I usually use incentives to lure kids into doing what they are supposed to do. Or I do a magic trick or show them something funny or use a puppet so that they want to come back to the group. I try using a firm voice and letting them know that, if they don't come back, they will lose a privilege (e.g., they will have to sit out when we are playing a game). Sometimes I tell them that they need to be on the carpet by the count of three. However, sometimes kids simply won't come to the carpet. As long as they are quiet and I can see them, I let them stay where they are.

Small children are naturally very touchy. They are very affectionate and love to hold hands and give hugs. They also use touch when they are frustrated and angry—hitting, biting, and kicking. A big part of helping Kindergarten students is teaching them how to share and how to resolve conflicts without resorting to physical means. It is good to remind them to treat other people the way that they want to be treated; I often ask children how they would feel if someone hit them. It is good to ask children to use their words to tell someone to stop doing something, instead of hitting them. Remind children that if they have told someone to stop and that person doesn't, they can come and get your help. It is also good to remind Kindergarten children that they need to ask the person to stop doing something before they come to get your help.

Academically

Kindergarten is the beginning of a child's education. Many children will not know very much at all when they arrive. Some Kindergarten children don't speak or understand English, as they have just arrived from another country or their parents do not speak English at home. It is amazing how quickly small children learn and how easily they adapt. It is more than possible for you to teach them many, many things in the course of just one day. This makes Kindergarten fun, interesting, and exciting—if not quiet!

Many children will not be able to read and will simply look at pictures in a book. At the beginning of Kindergarten, children are still learning which way is up when holding a book. They learn that sentences go from left to right, top to bottom. By the end of Kindergarten, many children will be able to read easy picture books—and there always seems to be one child who is already reading chapter books!

When children start Kindergarten, they are still learning how to hold a pencil and crayons, how to make straight lines, and how to write on the lines. Children learn to print their first names in Kindergarten. By the end of Kindergarten, many children can write simple sentences. Often a teacher scribes for the child and the child copies it. Other times the teacher writes in highlighter and the child writes over top of that in pencil.

Most children can count to 10 before they come to school; however, it is not uncommon for children to not know their numbers at all. By the end of Kindergarten, children not only can count to ten but also can look at the printed number and tell you what it is. They know that six is more than five and less than seven. Many children can count much higher than 10, with some even being able count to 100.

How to Teach Kindergarten Well

Kindergarten kids will eat you for lunch if you are not prepared for them! The key to success in teaching Kindergarten is to be firm. And to have some fun—there are other ways, but this is my favorite. In order to build relationships and make them feel safe, you need to be likable. For them to feel safe and for you to be sane, they need to know what the rules are and that they will be enforced.

Kindergarten children will test boundaries, rules, and limits. They will test them again and again and again. It is really important to be firm and to reinforce the rules and boundaries. This is where patience comes in. Kindergarten requires a lot of patience. It is very easy to lose a Kindergarten class to a case of the sillies and giggles. Remember, it is okay to have fun—even silly fun—as long as you are in control and they stop and listen and are quiet when you ask. If a student continues to act out, it is okay to have that child sit a bit away from the rest of the class until he or she is able to be quiet and listen.

You will probably have to remind the children at the beginning of the day (and all the way through the day) that they need to put up a hand if they want to talk. In Kindergarten, always answer the child who is frantically waving a hand: it may be the child needs to go to the bathroom—and Kindergarten kids sometimes need to go right away. If the kid doesn't need to go to the bathroom, he or she may just want to tell what happened to them one time. When a child starts off on a story, I cut him or her off and say that he or she can tell me the story at snack time/free time. Otherwise, I'll be there all day, as children tell you a story one by one and the rest of the kids fool around.

To get children's attention when they are chatting or not listening, you can start singing a song and they will all join in. "Twinkle, Twinkle Little Star," "The Alphabet Song," and "Jingle Bells" all work very well. I also use puppets or stuffed animals to get students' attention. If they have lost interest in what you are doing, simply use a puppet or stuffed animal to do the talking for you. It guarantees you will have their rapt attention then!

When all else fails, count. If children will not listen or do what you want, start counting and they will almost always fall in line. Of course, you have to stop counting eventually (around three or five). If a child has not done what you asked by then, that student needs to be placed alone, away from others. If the child will not stay there, I say I will be writing a note for his/her parents to read and then continue on with my lesson.

When Kindergarten children are not doing what you have told them to do, sometimes it is because they have just forgotten. Small children have very short attention spans and very little retention. That means they will easily forget what they are supposed to be doing. So it is good to give just one or two directions at a time. If you would like them to wash their hands, get their snack, and sit at the table, it is good simply to get everyone to wash their hands first. Then tell everyone to get their snack and sit at the table. It is important to remember to keep things very simple.

Schedules and consistency are important for Kindergarten children. As much as possible, I try to follow the schedule and routines they normally have. If there is an ECE (Early Childhood Educator) or an EA (Educational Assistant), he or she will know what to do and it makes the day much easier. Also, the children will be quick to tell you what you are supposed to do next. When this is not possible, I tell students that we will be doing something different from normal and that they will return to their regular routines when their teacher comes back.

If you are using humor to teach Kindergarteners, keep in mind that being silly is the preferred humor at this age:

- I have all the children sit down. Then I tell them to stand up. Then I pretend I forgot something and have them sit down. Then I say, "No, no, what are you doing? Stand up, stand up." I have them sit down and stand up a few more

Some teachers use the saying, "Hands on top…That means stop" to get children to place their hands on their heads to stop what they are doing. This is not always great for Kindergarten children, as they tend to have sand or glue or bugs in their hands when they touch their head. This may be a better strategy for Grades 1 or 2.

It is important to note that it is sometimes difficult to rein a Kindergarten class back in after being silly with them. It is more important that they have a calm day than that they have a fun day. If a class is too silly and too difficult to control, consider simply being kind and firm and leave being silly and having fun for another day.

times, at which point they are all laughing. Then I ask them if they are being silly and they all tell me no; I ask if I'm being silly and they tell me yes!

- When I read a book to a Kindergarten class, I stop halfway through and say it's too scary and that I can't read the rest. They all laugh or tell me they'll hold my hand. Sometimes I make up an ending halfway through: e.g., "And then Tommy the squirrel died. The end." The children all know this is not really the end and yell that out to me. I also pretend to fall asleep halfway through the book; they think this is hilarious.

Kindergarten Day Plan and Lessons

Kindergarten Day Plan: Building and Patterns

Starting Routines
    Self-Introduction/Attendance/Joke, Story, Fact, etc.: 10 minutes
    Silent Reading: 15 minutes
    Calendar: 10 minutes
Period 1: Language
    Introduce Language Activity: 5 minutes
    Language Activity: 15 minutes
    Take Up Language Activity: 10 minutes
    Language Game: 10 minutes
Snack: 15 Minutes
Period 2: Activity Centres
    Introduce Activity Centres: 5 minutes
    Activity Centres: 60 minutes
    Clean Up Activity Centres: 10 minutes
Lunch
Afternoon Routines
    Attendance/Joke, Story, Fact, etc.: 10 minutes
    Read a Book: 10 minutes
    Show and Tell: 15 minutes
Period 3: Math
    Introduce Math Activity: 5 minutes
    Math Activity: 15 minutes
    Take Up Math Activity: 10 minutes
    Math Game: 10 minutes
Snack: 15 minutes
Period 4: Science
    Introduce Science Activity: 5 minutes
    Science Activity: 40 minutes
    Take Up Science Activity: 10 minutes
    Clean Up Science Activity: 10 minutes
Get Ready to Go Home: 10 minutes
Home Time

Starting Routines

Self-Introduction/Attendance/Joke, Story, Fact, etc.

After you help children with buttons, shoes, etc., students will automatically start their routine. Some classes sit on the carpet; some read a book; others get out an agenda. It is important to stick to the students' regular schedule as much as possible—the children will make sure you know that. If you do not, they will tell you that you are not doing it right and will indicate that you are not a very good teacher.

The *special helper* will help you with the regular routine. This is a different student every day, and students usually know when it is their turn. The special helper is often the first person in line all day. He or she often leads the review of the days of the week and weather at the beginning of the day; helps hand out papers and take notes to the office. Often the special helper gets to wear a special hat or pin. By no means should you pick a different special helper. This is akin to your parents giving your inheritance to the next-door neighbor and not you, and will evoke a similar response. If students don't know who the special helper is that day, find out who was the special helper the day before and choose the student who is next in order on the attendance list.

Silent Reading

There are always books in a Kindergarten classroom. Allow children to pick a book and to read it quietly on the carpet (or at the tables, if they normally do that). Some classes have book bags and children have a specific book to read. If books are exchanged everyday, let children know that they will exchange books when their teacher is back and today they can read the same book. Allow children to read more than one book, as they might get bored if they try to read the same book for 15 minutes.

Calendar Time

Almost all Kindergarten classrooms have Calendar time. This is about 10 minutes during which children sing songs about the days of the week and the months of the year, count the number of days in the month, look at the weather outside, and perform a variety of other activities. It is not a problem that you do not know the songs, because the children will know them and will sing them—just say, "One, two, three, go!" The special helper or a child you choose can lead Calendar time, and it should go pretty smoothly with your guidance.

If it is the first week of school in a Junior Kindergarten class and children do not yet know the songs, you can have them repeat the days of the week after you, one by one: you say, "Sunday," and then the children say, "Sunday"; you say, "Monday," and then the children say, "Monday"; and so on. They can repeat the months of the year after you, one by one. They can count the number of days in the month so far with you. Then, you can ask the children what the weather is like outside. You can also ask what season it is.

Period 1: Language

Introduce Language Activity

1. Ask: *Have you ever seen people building things?*

2. Ask: *Have you ever seen the trucks that help build things? Do you know what the trucks are called?* Children may know the words for "dump truck," "crane," "loader," "bulldozer" or "digger."
3. Ask: *If you could build something, what would you build?* You may need to give suggestions, such as a house, bridge, school, or fire station.

Language Activity

See page 39 for the Kindergarten Language Activity sheet.

1. Show the Kindergarten Language Activity sheet (page 39) and tell students they are going to make a picture of what they would like to build. They are to label the parts as best they can; for example, they can label the windows and doors of a house.
2. Read the beginning of the two sentences at the bottom of the page. Tell students to tell what they drew in the first sentence and then tell one thing about it in the second sentence. For example, "I built a hospital. It is white."
3. Hand out the Kindergarten Language Activity sheet (page 39) and ask children to write their names at the top of the page. You might have to help some children with this.
4. Ask children to write the word or the first letter of the word if they can't write the whole word. If they cannot write at all, you can write words for the children in highlighter and then they can go over them in pencil.

Take Up Language Activity

1. Have the children come back to the carpet with their Kindergarten Language Activity sheets.
2. Ask one child to show the class his or her sheet. Ask that student to tell the class what he/she drew and one thing about his/her structure.
3. Allow each child to share with the class what he/she drew and one thing about the structure.
4. Collect the sheets to leave for the teacher.

Language Game

1. Have the children sit in a circle on the carpet.
2. Give one child a ball, a block, or a crumpled piece of paper. The children pass the ball around the circle until you say, "Stop." (Or play music and have the children pass the ball until you stop the music.)
3. The child holding the ball says his/her name and the first letter of the name. Then the student says one more word that starts with the same sound as his/her name. For example, Cathy would say, "Cathy. Cathy starts with a *C*. *Cat* also starts with *c*." (Note the child can identify the letter or the sound.)
4. The children pass the ball around until you say, "Stop" (or the music stops) and the game continues with the next child.

Snack

Children get their snack and go to the tables to eat. Make sure it's a snack and not their lunch. Kindergarten children might not know that a sandwich is lunch and the cheese and crackers are snack. In some classes, children wash their hands at the sink first or use hand sanitizer. Ask children to stay seated at the table and chat with their friends until snack time is over.

Period 2: Activity Centres

Introduce Activity Centres

Teachers often use a system by which each child has a card to put in an activity centre chart. That way, teachers can make sure only a certain number of children go to each centre, and can see who was using any centre that is not cleaned up at the end.

All Kindergarten rooms have activity centres. Common activity centres include the building/blocks centre, the house centre, the arts and crafts centre, the sand table, the water table, the painting centre, the reading centre, the math table, the language table, and computers. There is usually a limit to how many children can be at each centre: often four children at each centre, but only two at the painting centre, water table, sand table, and computers.

1. Tell children they will be allowed to go to activity centres.
2. Ask them to tell you the rules: they will say things like, "No pushing," and "Talk quietly." Ask them how many children are allowed at each centre. Ask them what do you do when you want to change centres.

Activity Centres

1. Call children one by one to choose a centre.
2. As students work at centres, monitor the class to make sure it does not get too loud and that the children are playing nicely with each other and the equipment.

Clean Up Activity Centres

1. Get the class's attention. Once students are all looking at you quietly, ask them if they have a clean-up song (many classes sing while they clean up). Whether they have a song or not, tell children it is time to clean up and you expect them all to clean up; those who finish first are to help others clean.
2. As they clean up, you will probably have to remind some children that it is clean-up time and that they are to help. After the children clean up, tell them it is time to get ready for lunch.

Lunch

Some children may go home for lunch. In that case, dismiss the children to a parent/guardian or an older sibling.

Kindergarten children usually eat in their own classroom. The ECE (Early Childhood Educator), EA (Educational Assistant), or lunch lady stays with them while you go to lunch. Often the teacher gets the children sitting quietly and eating before the lunch bell. In some classes, the children all wash their hands or use hand sanitizer before lunch.

Afternoon Routines

Attendance/Joke, Story, Fact, etc.

There is often a routine that Kindergarten children follow after lunch for attendance. If possible, follow the regular schedule. There is often a specific child or two who take the attendance to the office if there is no special helper assigned. If the children do not know whose turn it is, ask who took the attendance the day before and choose the next child on the attendance sheet.

Read a Book

Find a book in the Kindergarten classroom to read to the class. You can also get a book from the school library or from another teacher. Find a book that looks interesting—a book about building if you can find it—and read it to the class.

Before you read the book, show students the front of the book and ask them what they think the book is about. It is more interesting for the class if you use different voices for each character in the book. Partway through the book, stop and ask children what they think will happen at the end (tell them to answer only if they haven't read that book before). Read the end of the book and ask children what they think will happen to the characters after the book ends.

Show and Tell

Some classes have show and tell every day; children will know whose turn it is. In other classes, it is not strictly scheduled. In that case, the special helper can choose two friends or you can choose three people to show and tell. The three students can go to their bags and get something they would like to show the class. If they have nothing to show, they can tell the class something. When a child is done showing the class an object and telling about it, the other children can ask questions. I usually allow three questions.

Period 3: Math

Introduce Math Activity

1. Ask children if they know what a pattern is. If they do not know, tell them it is something that repeats.
2. Ask students to find a pattern in the classroom.
3. If they cannot find one, point one out. For example, usually at least one student is wearing stripes; show how the colors in the stripes repeat: e.g., red, white, red, white. Ask students to find more patterns in the room.

Math Activity

See page 40 for the Kindergarten Math Activity sheet.

1. Show the students the Kindergarten Math Activity page (page 40).
2. Say the first pattern together: "Square, circle, square, circle." Explain that students are to draw the next three shapes in the pattern. Tell them to do the same thing for all three patterns in number 1.
3. Point to the 100 chart and tell them to find the pattern of the squares that are colored in. Explain that they are to continue with the pattern and color in the squares up to 100.
4. Point to the first square and show how it is not colored in. Point to the next square and show how it is colored in. Ask if they can see the pattern.
5. Ask which square should be colored in next.
6. Explain that they are to make their own pattern for number 3.
7. Hand out the Kindergarten Math Activity sheets and have children take them to the tables.
8. Ask them to write their name on the page. You may need to help some children write their name.
9. As the children are doing the Math Activity, go around and help those who are having difficulty. You might need to read the directions to some children again.

Take Up Math Activity

See page 41 for Answer Key for Kindergarten Math Activity.

1. Have children come to the carpet.
2. Ask them to raise their hand if they know what shape comes next after the circle in the first part of number 1. Read the pattern together as a class. Do the same with all three patterns in number 1.

3. Ask children to raise their hand if they would like to show the class how they colored in their 100 chart. Allow a couple of children to show their charts to the class. (Try to pick children who did it correctly.)
4. Ask children who would like to show the pattern that they made up themselves. Allow a couple of children to show their pattern to the class. Collect the sheets for the teacher and leave with the answer key (page 41).

Math Game

Tell children they will walk around the carpet while you play music. When the music stops, you will call out a number from one to four. They are to get into groups containing as many students as the number you call out: if you call out *two*, they are to get into groups of two; if you call out *three*, they are to get into groups of three, etc. If you don't have music, children can simply walk around the carpet until you call out a number.

Snack

Children get their snack and go to the tables to eat. In some classes, children wash their hands at the sink first or use hand sanitizer. Some children might not have a snack left for afternoon recess. They can simply sit and chat with their friends at the table. Ask children to stay seated at the table and chat with their friends until snack time is over. Children are not usually allowed to share their snack as some children have severe allergies. By the way, have you had your EpiPen training yet?

Period 4: Science

Setting Up for Science

You will need about five minutes to set up for Science. Most Kindergarten classrooms have some materials that can be used for building. Often there are large blocks, small blocks, Lego, etc. Place the building materials around the classroom so that the children can work with them in groups of four and have enough room to build.

Introduce Building Activity

1. Ask children if they remember what they drew for the Language Activity in the morning. Ask if they think they could build that structure with the materials you have in the room.
2. Ask how they would build it.
3. Tell children that they are going to try their best to build that structure now.

Building Activity

1. Divide children into groups of four. Have each group of four work at one of the building stations you set up. Children can build their own structures individually, or they can work with their group to build a structure together. Or some students in the group can work on their own structures and some can work together.
2. Remind them that the blocks are for building and not for throwing. If you see anyone throwing blocks, they will be asked to sit out for a while.
3. If children tell you they have finished before the time is up, encourage them to take their structure down and build another structure. If they have worked alone, encourage them to work with the group. If they worked with

the group, encourage them to try to build something by themselves. If everyone is finished early, consider having the groups rotate to another building station to use different building materials.

Take Up Building Activity

1. Have children sit with their hands in their laps where they are. Make sure they are sitting so they can see you.
2. Ask who would like to share what they have built with the class. Ask the child to describe the structure.
3. Have a few children share what they built.

Clean Up

See page 34.

Get Ready to Go Home

In the winter, Kindergarten children need extra time to put on all their clothes. It will take about 20 minutes—I am not exaggerating. In warmer weather, 10 to 15 minutes should be enough. Remind children to take their lunch bags, scarves, hats, mitts, letters from the school, agendas, backpacks, and the kitchen sink.

Kindergarten children can be allowed out the door only when a parent/guardian is there to pick them up at dismissal time. This is usually true for all children in Grade 3 and under. They will tell you—quite excitedly—when they see their mom, dad, grandma, daycare worker, gorilla, or whoever is picking them up.

Extra Activities and Games

You might find you have extra time, because the children cleaned up so quickly. Or you may decide to cut short an activity if children are having a hard time focusing and staying seated. In this case, here are a couple of games and activities to use.

Singing

Kindergarten children love to sing. You can sing all of the very easy, preschool songs and they will love it. Some examples: "The Alphabet Song," "Twinkle, Twinkle, Little Star," "Baa, Baa, Black Sheep," "Head and Shoulders," "The Wheels on the Bus," or any nursery rhyme. You can also ask children what song they want to sing of the ones they usually sing in class. Even if you don't know it, you can simply ask a child to start singing and the other children will join in.

Duck, Duck, Goose

This game requires a bit of space. Many Kindergarten classrooms will have enough space to play this game on the carpet.

- Children sit in a circle. One child is It.
- The child who is It walks around the outside of the circle, tapping children on the head and saying, "Duck" with every tap.
- Then one time instead of "Duck," it is "Goose." The child who is It starts to run all the way around the outside of the circle and sits down in the Goose's spot. The child who is the Goose chases the child who is It around the outside of the circle, trying to catch and touch that child.
- The Goose is now It and walks around the circle, repeating the game.

Sometimes the Goose runs the opposite way around from the child who is It and tries to beat It back to the spot. I find that this creates crashes in the classroom; a gym is preferable to a classroom to play like this.

- The game continues on until everyone has had a turn to be Goose or time is up.

I Spy

- Pick something in the classroom without revealing what it is. Say, "I spy with my little eye, something that is (the color of the chosen object)."
- Children put up their hands to guess the item you have picked.
- When a child guesses correctly, they get to do the spying. That child says, "I spy with my little eye something that is (the color of something in the classroom)."
- After repeating a few times, children can break into partners or groups of three and play the game together so that everyone has a chance to say, "I spy…"

Kindergarten Language Activity

Name: _____ Date: _____

Draw a picture of something you would like to build. Label the parts.

I built a _____

It is _____

Kindergarten Math Activity

Name:_____ Date: _____

1. Finish the pattern.

2. Finish the pattern by coloring in the boxes.

1	2	3	4	5	6	7	8	9	10
11	12	13	14	15	16	17	18	19	20
21	22	23	24	25	26	27	28	29	30
31	32	33	34	35	36	37	38	39	40
41	42	43	44	45	46	47	48	49	50
51	52	53	54	55	56	57	58	59	60
61	62	63	64	65	66	67	68	69	70
71	72	73	74	75	76	77	78	79	80
81	82	83	84	85	86	87	88	89	90
91	92	93	94	95	96	97	98	99	100

1	2	3	4	5	6	7	8	9	10
11	12	13	14	15	16	17	18	19	20
21	22	23	24	25	26	27	28	29	30
31	32	33	34	35	36	37	38	39	40
41	42	43	44	45	46	47	48	49	50
51	52	53	54	55	56	57	58	59	60
61	62	63	64	65	66	67	68	69	70
71	72	73	74	75	76	77	78	79	80
81	82	83	84	85	86	87	88	89	90
91	92	93	94	95	96	97	98	99	100

3. Make your own pattern.

_____ _____ _____   _____ _____ _____

Pembroke Publishers ©2016 *Substitute Teaching?* by Amanda Yuill ISBN 978-1-55138-312-5

Answer Key for Kindergarten Math Activity

1.

2. Finish the pattern by coloring in the boxes.

1	2	3	4	5	6	7	8	9	10
11	12	13	14	15	16	17	18	19	20
21	22	23	24	25	26	27	28	29	30
31	32	33	34	35	36	37	38	39	40
41	42	43	44	45	46	47	48	49	50
51	52	53	54	55	56	57	58	59	60
61	62	63	64	65	66	67	68	69	70
71	72	73	74	75	76	77	78	79	80
81	82	83	84	85	86	87	88	89	90
91	92	93	94	95	96	97	98	99	100

1	2	3	4	5	6	7	8	9	10
11	12	13	14	15	16	17	18	19	20
21	22	23	24	25	26	27	28	29	30
31	32	33	34	35	36	37	38	39	40
41	42	43	44	45	46	47	48	49	50
51	52	53	54	55	56	57	58	59	60
61	62	63	64	65	66	67	68	69	70
71	72	73	74	75	76	77	78	79	80
81	82	83	84	85	86	87	88	89	90
91	92	93	94	95	96	97	98	99	100

3. Answers will vary.

4

Substitute Teaching Primary Grades

Grade 1: Can I Hold Your Hand?

One little girl in Grade 1 knew Santa Claus wasn't real. Her father had told her so. She was trying to convince the rest of the class that Santa Claus wasn't real. I called her over to my desk.

"Who told you Santa Claus isn't real?" I asked.

"My dad," she said.

"And who should tell the other kids Santa Claus isn't real?" I asked.

"Their dads," she said.

"That's right," I said. "I don't want you telling the other kids that Santa isn't real."

But she did anyway. The other kids got really angry, ganged up on her, and made her cry; thus establishing that Santa Claus is, in fact, real. The class then went on to discuss if Santa Claus and the Tooth Fairy were the same person. They decided they were not the same person because Santa Claus brings presents and the Tooth Fairy brings money.

What Grade 1 Students Are Like

Physically

Grade 1 students still need quite a bit of help. They often cannot use scissors very well at the beginning of the school year. They need help with buttons and zippers and boots. They need help reading, writing, and using their fingers or counters to do math. It's a physical job teaching Grade 1! You are on your feet a lot of the time.

The need to move around is inherent in Grade 1 students. They find it difficult to sit still longer than five minutes—especially if they are simply listening. Even when they are doing an activity they enjoy, like coloring or playing a game, some students will have a hard time sitting still.

Grade 1 students are always losing teeth and, when one falls out, they expect you to pick it up and put it in a tissue securely enough that they can get it home to the tooth fairy! Everyone knows you have to put it under your pillow or you don't get any money. Kids get a lot of money from the Tooth Fairy these days. I often ask if I can keep the tooth because I need the money!

Grade 1 students sometimes throw up all over the room. The important thing is to keep other students away from the mess and to help the child as quickly as possible. Keep the child near the sink or garbage can. Call the office as soon as possible and ask them to send the caretaker to clean it up. The office will send someone to get the child, or you can send the child with a friend to the office where his/her parents will be called. Be sure to tell the other children not to laugh at the child who was sick. Most important is to wash your hands thoroughly afterwards!!

Grade 1 students sometimes have accidents in their pants; not as often as Kindergartners, but often enough that some of them will have extra clothes in their backpacks. If a child does have an accident, don't draw attention to it and don't let other students make fun of the child. If the child has extra clothes, send them to the bathroom to change. If not, send the child with a note to the office, where they often keep extra clothes or where the child's parents will be called to bring a change of clothes.

Socially

Grade 1 students want to hold your hand. They give hugs—they will hug your leg before you even know what's happening! They are physical and affectionate and sweet and cute. They don't really get sarcasm though… One of the absolute best things about Grade 1 students is that they really want your approval. They care what you think about them! This makes it easier to teach them, because they are more likely to do what you ask, especially if the request is said in a firm voice.

Grade 1 children want your undivided attention. Who cares that there are nineteen other students? Students get up out of their seats and pull on your sleeve to get your attention if you don't give it to them when they raise their hand. You need to remind them (ad nauseum) to sit down and put up their hands. They want you to know about themselves. They want to tell you what they did yesterday and what their dad did yesterday and why their aunt is sick and so on.

Besides your attention, they also want to be the first in line or the first done; they will have great, dramatic arguments about who was actually first. They will rush to be the first done, to the detriment of their work. To stop this, I give an incentive to students who are doing their work well. Some teachers will have a *line order*, a specific order in which students stand so that they don't run into the line and into each other. If there are lots of problems with pushing and butting in line, I tell them to stand in line order; if their teacher is anything like me, students will start moving to their spots in line. If they don't have a line order, I have the boys line up first, then the girls. The end of the line tends to be noisier and bouncier than the front, so I try to keep the bounciest boys and girls up front.

Everything is a big deal in Grade 1. When somebody bumps into them accidentally, they are sure it was on purpose. Their archenemy stole their pencil! They have a hard time putting themselves in another person's shoes to see that it was not all an evil plot against them personally.

Academically

Grade 1 students change quite a bit during the year. They learn a lot of things in Grade 1, the most important being how to read. To see the average spectrum, consider these things Grade 1 students can do at the beginning of the year and at the end of the year.

At the beginning of the year, Grade 1 students can

- often read only books that are very repetitive, with only one word changing per page: e.g., *The boot is yellow. / The hat is yellow. / The coat is yellow.*
- write the first letter of a word and final consonant.
- add on their fingers (so up to 5 + 5) and count to 20.
- follow one or two directions at a time.

By the end of the year, Grade 1 students can
- often read most simple sentences: e.g., Robert Munsch books.
- sound out short words phonetically.
- write the beginning, middle, and end sounds of a word.
- add up to 10 + 10 and count to 100.
- follow two or three simple directions at a time (but everything will take 1.5 times as long as you think it will).

How to Teach Grade 1 Well

Every once in a while, primary children need to move around—sometimes just to avoid falling asleep. They will get more difficult to handle if they have been sitting quietly and still for too long. If this happens, have everyone stand up and we do a couple of minutes of exercises: ten jumping jacks, running on the spot, jumping to touch the ceiling (I tell them that they haven't touched the ceiling yet, so we're going to keep on trying), etc.

Sometimes it is difficult to get Grade 1 students' attention because they are so busy coloring their picture, talking with a friend, or arguing over whose pencil it is. It is helpful to have a few different ideas for attention-getters.
- At the beginning of the day, establish that when you turn the lights off and on, they will stop talking.
- Teach them that when you say, "Hands on top…", they put their hands on their heads and reply with, "…That means stop." This is effective because even if the children stop talking, they often continue coloring or grabbing a pencil from their friend. With their hands on their heads, they are much more likely to look at you and listen.
- Singing works. You can start to sing a song and they will join in. When the song is done, you can give instructions.
- If you use a loud voice to get their attention, speak more and more quietly, and this will cause them to be very quiet to hear you.
- Arrange with students that when you count down from five, they need to be quiet when you get to zero. People who are still talking when you get to zero will have to put their hands on their heads to remind them to listen well.

Grade 1 students love slapstick humor and silliness. The key is to use the kind of humor they respond to without letting the class get out of control. I often have children make monkey faces or fish faces in between activities or when we first get to the carpet. Or sometimes I talk in a silly, high voice and then a really deep voice. When I'm reading the directions for an activity, I end off with, "…and then give Ms. Yuill your lunch so she can eat it because she is very hungry." Be sure to assure them you are just teasing!

You will hear common complaints in Grade 1 that you will be answering over and over:
- When a little girl comes to you at recess and says, "The boys are bothering me," say, "Tell the boys, 'My mother says that when a boy bothers you, it

means he likes you.' He'll never bother you again!" (Same thing in reverse for boys; with boys this works up to the middle of Grade 6).

- When a child complains that another kid hit him/her on purpose and the other child says it was an accident, ask the supposed batterer if he/she apologized. If the kid says, "Yes, over and over," then it really was an accident. If the kid says, "No, because I didn't mean to," it was on purpose. Anyone who hits someone else by accident apologizes right away because they feel bad. Anyone who means to hit someone apologizes only to get out of trouble!

It is really important to be firm as soon as inappropriate behavior starts. If you are having fun and the class starts getting out of control, use one of the attention-getters on pages 9–10 and use a firm voice. It is important to stop inappropriate behavior as soon as it starts or it will run rampant in a Grade 1 class! Hesitation is the crack in the dam of hyper-silliness! He/she who hesitates to stop it is lost in the sea of giggling children running around in circles.

It often seems as if Grade 1 students have understood all your instructions when really they understood nothing. It's always helpful to have students repeat instructions before starting an activity or going back to their desks after being on the carpet. Ask one or two students to repeat the instructions. Then ask the whole class to repeat the instructions. Try not to be too surprised when half the class still doesn't do what was clearly repeated several times in the instructions.

Everything will take a long time. However long you think an activity should take, plan twice as much time and twice as much patience. They really aren't trying to drive you insane on purpose. It's just their natural way!

Grade 2: I'm Not Your Friend!

Me: Please draw a picture with your family and label it.
Grade 2 Boy: Ms. Yuill, how do you spell *iguana*?
Me: Oh, do you have an iguana at home?
Grade 2 Boy: No, it died.
End Result: Picture of his family with the dead iguana and only the iguana is labelled.

What Grade 2 Students Are Like

Physically

Grade 2 students may still need help tying their shoelaces and turning the arms of their coats right-side out. The teeth continue to fall out and they continue to rake in the dough! They can still have bathroom accidents or throw up. When this happens, call the office to let them know what has happened so a caretaker can come and clean up the mess. Send the child with a friend to the office. You might need to take your class to another room while the caretaker cleans the mess and airs out the classroom a bit. You can see if the library is free or if the teacher there would mind if your class joined them. You can also take students outside if it is a nice day. Sometimes I just take the students on a little tour of the school.

You can often tell if a child is seriously sick if he/she is pale, has a hot forehead, or falls asleep at his/her desk.

Sometimes a Grade 2 student will say that his/her stomach, or head, or leg, or arm hurts…you get the picture. If it is the stomach that hurts, ask them to try to go to the bathroom and see if that helps. If it is the head, ask them to get a drink of water. If somewhere on the body hurts, ask if they want a bandage. If worse comes to worst, you can send the student to the office for ice. Ice is magic in primary classes and makes all manner of hurts better.

Socially

Be sure to have lots of tissues. Grade 2 kids have issues with friends—a lot. It's like a regular soap opera if you allow them to tell you the whole story. I can sometimes hear the elevator music in the background as a Grade 2 kid sobs out the story. Okay, I admit that it isn't that different from grown-ups sometimes. You may feel you're more a referee than anything else. Of course, this can be true with a Grade 8 class too, especially in the spring! I usually say, "Tell them to stop it and to say they are sorry."

Grade 2 kids have cliques or clubs. They are exclusive clubs. Kids who are not invited into the clubs are very sad. Kids who were in the club but got kicked out are even sadder. I tell Grade 2 students I don't want to hear, "You're not my friend." Instead, I want to hear, "I'm angry with you." I sometimes have discussions about how you can be angry at friends and still be friends with them, a concept some 30-year-olds still haven't mastered. In Grade 2, they still need to be reminded that you don't have to play with your best friend all the time. And if your best friend doesn't play with you one recess, this does not mean he or she is not your friend. This needs to be repeated a thousand times per day. It's also necessary to tell students that just because someone doesn't want to share with you doesn't mean that person is not your friend. It's important to stress that children don't have to share their own things with others, even if the other person asked nicely. (Have I inspired you to go and get your lawnmower back?)

Grade 2 students want you to like them and they will like you. Rebellious behavior is not usually the problem. Not having enough attention to go around while you help everyone who needs help and referee fights is the problem.

Academically

Grade 2 students' abilities change quite a bit during the year. To see the average spectrum, consider these things Grade 2 students can do at the beginning of the year and at the end of the year.

At the beginning of the year, Grade 2 students can
- read books that have simple sentences with easy or common words.
- sound out short words phonetically.
- write simple sentences.
- write the beginning, middle, and end sounds in a word and some common words.
- count to 100 and add up to 10 + 10.
- follow two or three directions at a time.

By the end of the year, Grade 2 students can
- read easy chapter books.
- figure out words that have a vowel–consonant–letter *e* pattern, along with some other common patterns.
- write longer sentences and use periods and capitals properly.
- follow a few directions at time.

How to Teach Grade 2 Well

Grade 2 students will need to move every ten minutes after listening to instructions, or every 20 minutes if they are doing an activity. It can be as simple as getting a drink or moving from the carpet to their desks. If students are antsy, you can sing a song that involves movement or do a game; e.g., Simon Says or some quick exercises.

It is amazing how loud Grade 2 children can be! Sometimes I think it is not physically safe for your hearing to be around the amount of noise they are able to generate for the whole day! It is good to have a few attention-getting strategies that don't always involve a loud voice:

- Say, "If you can hear me, touch your nose. If you can hear me, touch your arm." Continue on with different body parts. More and more children will do what you are asking and eventually the whole class will be listening to you.
- Arrange with the class that when you clap a pattern, they will clap back the same pattern. As you clap different patterns, more and more children will be listening until the whole class is clapping a pattern and you can go on with your instructions.

Grade 2 students are still into silly, slapstick humor. Toilet humor is also very funny to them. Really, all the way up to Grade 8 they laugh at feces (and perhaps you do, too). I tell gross facts about how dung beetles eat feces. They love that stuff!

Sometimes it takes a long time for Grade 2 students to say what they want to say. They put up their hands to answer the question and just when you think they have forgotten, they start to talk. Spelling the word "cat" can take 30 seconds that feels like all afternoon! Remember to pack your patience.

Grade 3: That's Not Fair!

Grade 3 Boy: Ms. Yuill, you don't look so good.
Other Grade 3 Boy: I know what it is. It's her hair, isn't it?

Grade 3 Girl: Ms. Yuill, why aren't you married yet? You're so pretty.
Me: Why? Are all the pretty teachers married?
Grade 3 Girl: Well…
Me: All the pretty ones my age are married?
Grade 3 Girl: Yes!!

What Grade 3 Students Are Like

Physically

Grade 3 students are usually able to sit still for a 20-minute lesson and do their work quietly at their desk for 20–30 minutes. In the afternoon, they tend to be more antsy than the morning, and may need to move around a bit more.

Some Grade 3 girls are already starting to go through puberty. Yes, it's young, but it happens often enough to make mention of it. Grade 3 boys have no idea how to handle this and sometimes make inappropriate comments about girls' bodies. It's important to let students know that this is not okay, while keeping in mind that they don't know any better.

Grade 3 students are still losing teeth (does it ever stop?). However, they are more able to put the teeth away safely themselves. You can usually send them to the office to get little resealable plastic bags to help them keep teeth safe until they get them home to their pillow.

Socially

"That's not fair" is the battle cry of Grade 3 students! Everything must be fair. You must allow them to be first in line, to answer the question, etc., or you will be accused of being unfair. In their eyes, this is akin to being put on Santa's Naughty list. Being called unfair is the biggest insult a Grade 3 student can give a teacher. They are very conscious of justice—by that, I mean justice for themselves!

Everything seems to be really important when you are in Grade 3. If you have a fight with a friend, you are no longer friends. If someone bumps into you, that person punched you on purpose. Grade 3 students need help seeing that sometimes things happen by accident or that you can argue with a friend and still be friends.

Grade 3 students will come to the teacher to resolve an issue instead of trying to resolve it themselves. I often ask students if they have talked to the person who hurt them and asked them to apologize. If they have not, I send them back to that person to ask for an apology. If that person will not apologize, I find out what happened. Sometimes no apology is needed. Sometimes the child accused of hurting will tell me he/she didn't mean to hurt the other student. In that case, I ask the student to say, "I didn't mean to do that—sorry." Students who really didn't mean to do it will apologize quickly. Students who did mean to do it will have a hard time apologizing!

Academically

Grade 3 students can
- read chapter books.
- write compound sentences using transitional words and appropriate punctuation.
- add and subtract double-digit numbers with regrouping.
- learn their multiplication facts throughout the year.
- do two-step problem solving.

How to Teach Grade 3 Well

Grade 3 students are starting to understand jokes. They love Knock, Knock jokes, why-did-the-chicken-cross-the-road jokes, and word jokes. There are many books and websites full of jokes for elementary-school children. Having a few jokes up your sleeve will make you the ever-popular substitute teacher. The children are also more than willing to share their jokes with the class! Of course, toilet and slapstick humor are still very much appreciated. If you pretend to knock the eraser off the ledge or pretend to keep dropping the chalk, they will think this is hilarious! Of course, once you start the giggles, beware—they might not stop!

Helping Grade 3 students deal with conflict resolution and stand up for themselves is really important. I tell students that they can ask me for help only if they have already spoken to the other person first. The question, "Did you talk to the other person?" keeps me from acting as referee instead of teacher all day.

It is still important to use a variety of techniques to get the attention of the class in Grade 3. Some teachers have a bell or chime on their desk to ring when they want the children to pay attention; if the teacher has one, use it, as the children are used to it. Clapping a pattern and having the children clap it back also works well. I sometimes ask the children what their teacher does and then use the same technique—no need to reinvent the wheel!

Primary Day Plan and Lessons

Primary Day Plan: Forces and Superheroes

Starting Routines
    Self-Introduction/Attendance/Joke, Story, Fact, etc.: 10 minutes
    Silent Reading: 15 minutes
Period 1: Language
    Introduce Cloze Activity: 5 minutes
    Cloze Activity: 5 minutes
    Introduce Language Activity: 5 minutes
    Language Activity: 10 minutes
    Introduce Writing Activity: 5 minutes
    Writing Activity: 15 minutes
    * Optional: Students who finish early can do the extra language activities. These can be used at any time students are finished work early during the day.
Get Ready for Recess: 5 minutes; 15 minutes in winter
Recess
Period 2: Math
    Math Game: 15 minutes
    Introduce Math Sheet: 5 minutes
    Math Sheet: 40 minutes
    Take Up Math Sheet: 10 minutes
Get Ready for Lunch: 5 minutes
Lunch
Afternoon Routines
    Attendance/Joke, Story, Fact, etc.: 10 minutes
Period 3: Science
    Introduce Science Experiment: 10 minutes
    Science Experiment: 40 minutes
    Take Up Science Experiment: 10 minutes
Get Ready for Recess: 5 minutes; 15 minutes in winter
Recess
Period 4: Art
    Introduce Art Activity: 10 minutes
    Art Activity: 50 minutes
Clean Up Classroom/Get Ready to Go Home: 15 minutes
Home Time

Starting Routines

Self-Introduction/Attendance/Joke, Story, Fact, etc.

Students in Grades 1 and 2 feel the most comfortable when they can follow a routine they know. The children will let you know what they do next, who takes the attendance to the office, what the consequences are for talking out, etc. I try to use what they know as much as I can. This makes them happy and easier to handle—and so I'm glad to do it!!

Scary stories and gross facts are a big hit with Grade 3 students. I tell only scary stories that aren't actually very scary, because some will still have nightmares if they listen to something really scary. Grade 3 students still like routine, but they are more flexible and able to go with the flow if you do things a bit differently than their teacher. They still think you are doing it the "wrong" way, though, and will tell you!

Silent Reading

Students will often already have a book they are reading. If they do not, let them pick one of the classroom books, while reminding them to put it back neatly where they got it from when we are finished.

- Some Grade 1 students cannot yet read and so they just look at the pictures. If Grade 1 students get restless quickly, you may want to read them a book.
- Most Grade 2 students can read a book on their own and are able to read for 10–15 minutes at a time. I encourage students to just pick one book they will read the whole time. If they get a bit antsy, I let them choose a different book for the last 5 minutes.
- Let Grade 3 students know that you expect them to read one book quietly for the whole 15 minutes.

Period 1: Language

Introduce Cloze Activity

1. Write the word *Forces* on the board. Tell students that a force is a push or a pull.
2. Ask them if they can think of something that can push or pull. As they tell you, write the name of the force on the board. For example, when they say people can push or pull, write *muscular force*. Other forces include: *gravity*, e.g., a ball dropping; *friction*, e.g., bicycle brakes; *magnetic force*, e.g., a magnet picking up a safety pin; *electrostatic force*, e.g., a balloon attracting your hair.
3. Talk about examples of forces.
   - Grade 1: You will probably have to give many hints, or you may just tell them about the different kinds of forces.
   - Grade 2: You can give examples of forces and ask students what they think is causing the push or pull: e.g., "Socks are often stuck together after being in the dryer. What do you think causes that?"
   - Grade 3: Write the rest of the words from the Cloze Activity on the board: *push*, *pull*, *speed*, *load*, and *distance*. Ask students what these words mean.

Cloze Activity

See page 60 for the Primary Cloze Activity sheet; page 61 for Answer Key for Primary Cloze Activity.

1. Show the students the Primary Cloze Activity sheet (page 60) with the list of words to use and the boxes showing where the words go. Explain that every box is a letter. Show them how the boxes show which letters go on the line, which letters go below the line, and which letters go above the line.
   - Grade 2: Show them how some words are short and some are long; have them count the number of boxes and the number of letters in a word.

The Cloze Activity may take all of the 20 minutes for the Cloze and Language Activities; you can skip the Language Activity and go straight to the Writing Activity. For Grade 2, you can choose to do the Language activity and skip the Cloze Activity.

Show them how sometimes there are two words side-by-side; have them look for two words side-by-side in the list of words.

- Grade 3: Explain that the word they pick to go in the box has to make sense in the sentence and fit the boxes.

2. Hand out the Cloze Activity Sheet and ask students to write their name on the paper.

3. Do an example together.
   - Grades 1 and 2: Do numbers one and two together, counting the letters to figure out which word goes in the boxes. Make sure the word fits.
   - Grade 3: Do number one together, showing how the word makes sense in the sentence and fits the box.

4. Allow students to do the rest by themselves.
   - Grade 1: If students understand, let them do the rest themselves. If they don't understand, this can be done as a whole-class activity. If the activity is too difficult, you may want to leave it and go on to the Language Activity Sheet.
   - Grade 2: Allow students to do the rest by themselves or in partners.

5. Collect the sheets for the teacher and leave with the answer key (page 61).

Introduce Language Activity

See page 62 for the Primary Language Activity sheet; see margin of page 53 for Answer Key for Primary Language Activity.

1. Hand out the Primary Language Activity sheet (page 62) and ask students to write their name on it.

2. Put words in alphabetical order.
   - Grade 1 students have not yet learned alphabetical order. Ask students to look at the first letter of each of the words in the list. Ask them to find the letter that is the closest to the beginning of the alphabet. When they find it, write it on the board. Now ask them to find the letter that is closest to the end of the alphabet. Write this on the board too.
   - Grade 2: Ask students which word starts with the letter closest to the start of the alphabet. Write that word on the board and ask them what they think it means. If they cannot guess, tell them the meaning of the word. Ask students which word starts with the letter that is next closest to the beginning of the alphabet. Write that word on the board and ask them the meaning of that word, helping and giving hints if they don't know. Continue with all the words.
   - Grade 3: Explain that ABC order means that they look at the first letter of each word and write the word that is closest to the beginning of the alphabet first; the word that starts with the letter next closest to the beginning of the alphabet goes second; etc. Together, find the word with the first letter closest to the beginning of the alphabet. Then find the word with the first letter that is next. Let students know they can continue this on their own.

Language Activity

1. Use words in a sentence.
   - Grade 1: Ask students to use as many of the words as they can in a sentence. Explain that if they don't know how to spell a word, they can just write the first letter. Do one sentence together; e.g., *I push my car.*
   - Grade 2: Read the directions for #2 and #3 as a class. Ask students to write a sentence with each word. If they need help, you can write one simple sentence together; e.g., *I like magnets.* If students don't know how to spell a word, they can sound it out using the first, middle, and end sounds. Ask

them to start with sentences for words that are easy; you can help them with the more difficult words.

- Grade 3: Read the directions for #2 and #3 as a class. Ask students to write a neat sentence with each word. Ask them to make sure they start with a capital and end with a period.

2. When they finish, they can draw pictures showing each word on the back of the page.

- Grade 1 students can draw pictures of the words they know. You will have to read the words for some of the students so they know what to draw.

Answer Key for Primary Language Activity
Distance, electrostatic force, force, friction, gravity, load, magnet, muscular force, pull, push, speed

Introduce Writing Activity

1. Ask about superheroes.
   - Grades 1 and 2: Ask: *If you were a superhero, what kind of super power would you have?*
   - Grade 3: Ask students who their favorite superhero is.
2. Relate super powers to forces.
   - Grades 1 and 2: Explain that super powers are often an example of a force; for example, super strength and super speed are examples of muscular force; shooting lightning bolts is electrostatic force.
   - Grade 3: Ask if they can think of a super power that uses a force; for example, super strength is muscular force; shooting lightning bolts is electrostatic force.

Writing Activity

See page 63 for the Primary Writing Activity sheet.

1. Hand out the Primary Writing Activity sheet (page 63) and ask students to write their name on it.
2. Have students write about super powers; i.e., forces.
   - Grades 1 and 2: Ask students to write about what kind of superhero they would like to be and what kind of super powers they would like to have. After writing, they can draw a picture.
   - Grade 1: Remind students that if they don't know how to write a word, they can write just the first letter of the word or sound it out.
   - Grade 2: Ask students what they would do with their super powers. Remind them that if they don't know how to spell a word, they can write the beginning, middle, and end sounds of that word.
   - Grade 3: Ask: *If you had to pick a super power using one of the forces we talked about* (you may need to review the forces), *which one would you pick?* Ask what they would do with that superpower.

Extra Language Activities

Word Search

See page 64 for the Extra Language Activity: Primary Word Search; page 65 for the Answer Key for Primary Word Search.

Give out the Extra Language Activity: Primary Word Search sheet (page 64) and ask students to write their name on it. Explain that the words at the bottom are hidden in the letters. Find one word together and show them how to circle it or highlight it.

Crossword

See page 66 for the Extra Language Activity: Primary Crossword; page 54 for the Answer Key for Primary Crossword.

Hand out the Extra Language Activity: Primary Crossword sheet (page 66) and ask students to write their name on it. Explain that just like the Cloze Activity, each box is for one letter. They can figure out which word goes where by counting the letters. Do one word together.

- Grades 2 and 3: Explain that the hints can help them figure out which word to use.

ANSWER KEY FOR PRIMARY CROSSWORD

Across	Down
2. Speed	1. Distance
4. Gravity	3. Muscular
5. Force	5. Friction
6. Electrostatic	7. Mass
7. Magnet	8. Pull
8. Push	

Get Ready for Recess

Remind students to take their snack and to wear all of the clothes their parents sent them with outside—coats, snow pants, boots or outdoor shoes, hats, mitts, etc. Grade 1 and 2 students will often go outside without their coat—even in winter!

- Grade 1: Make sure the coats are done up; some students may need help with this.
- Grade 2: You might want to check the coatrack to make sure they all took their coats.
- Grade 3: They can tie their coats around their waists if they are too hot.

For Grades 1 and 2, this will take 15 minutes in winter; for Grade 3, it will take 10 minutes in winter.

Period 2: Math

Math Game: Around the World

1. Have students sit at their desks. Pick one student to stand beside another student.
2. Ask an easy math addition fact. If the classroom has flash cards, use the flash cards.
   - Grade 1: An addition fact up to 5 + 5; e.g., 2 + 2.
   - Grade 2: An addition fact up to 10 + 10; e.g., 5 + 7.
   - Grade 3: An addition fact up to 10 + 10 or a subtraction fact from 20 − 10 to 1 − 1; at the end of the year, a multiplication fact up to 10 x 10.
3. If the student standing answers correctly first, they move on and stand beside the next student. If the student sitting answers correctly first, the standing student sits in that seat and the sitting student goes to the stand beside the next student.
4. Ask another addition fact and the game continues on.

Introduce Math Sheet

See pages 67–68 for the Primary Math Sheet.

Use the Primary Math Sheet (pages 67–68).
- Grade 1: Talk about the symbols for adding and subtracting. Write a plus sign and a minus sign on the board. Talk about patterns. Show a couple of patterns on the board; e.g., blue, green, blue, green. If there is a 100s chart in the room, show patterns on the 100 chart; e.g. 10, 20, 30.
- Grade 2: Word problems can still be difficult for Grade 2 students. Read one of the word problems at the bottom of the math sheet. Ask students if the words "all together" in a word problem means they will add or subtract. Ask if the word "left" means they will add or subtract. Do one of the word problems together on the board.

- Grade 3: On the board, write a couple of double-digit addition questions that involve regrouping; e.g., 35 + 26 or 84 + 9. Ask students if they start adding in the 10s column or the 1s column. Ask students what they do if the 1s column adds up to 10 or more. Have a student come to the board and show how to do the first example (giving help if needed). Have another student come up to show how to do the second example.

Math Sheet

1. Hand out the Primary Math Sheet (pages 67–68) and ask students to write their name on it.
   Grade 1: Read the instructions.
   Grade 2: Read the instructions together.
2. You may want to start with the Favorite Colors chart and do it at the beginning so everyone is up and asking each other questions at the same time.
3. Encourage students to do as much as they can on their own.
   - Grade 1: If some children are having difficulty doing anything, they can work with partners. You may have to read the problems to some of the students, so you can do these together at the end.
   - Grade 2: The students may not remember how to regroup; encourage students to do as many questions as they can by themselves.
   - Grade 3: After giving students 5 minutes to ask each other their favorite color, ask them to sit down and carry on with the rest of the sheet by themselves.

Take Up Math Sheet

See page 69 for the Answer Key for Primary Math Sheet.

- Grade 1: Ask students what answer they got for each question. Allow them to raise their hands and to answer when you call on them. Allow students to show their patterns and chart.
- Grade 2: Ask students if there were any questions they found really difficult. Do those questions together on the board. This may be a good opportunity to go over regrouping.
- Grade 3: Tell students that you are going to go around the classroom, getting everyone to answer questions. Point to one student; read out the first question and get the student to give his/her answer. Point to the next student; read out the next question and get the student to answer. Continue on until all the questions are answered. Or you can write the questions on the board and have students come up and write their answers.

Get Ready for Lunch

For Afternoon Routines, Grade 3 students love knock-knock jokes. Here is a classic:
A: Knock, knock.
B: Who's there?
A: Boo.
B: Boo who?
A: Oh, don't cry!

Remember to remind students to take everything with them. If students are going home for lunch, be sure to dismiss them to an adult. If you have students who are not picked up after 5 minutes, take them to the office to wait for their parents/guardian.

Period 3: Science

Setting Up for Science

You will need about 5 minutes to set up for the science experiment. Gather paper clips, erasers, pencils, pieces of paper, magnets, and elastics. Magnets are often found on the blackboard or on the fridge in the staff room. If there are no magnets or elastics available, use electrostatic force as your other force. Students can simply rub the objects on their clothes to cause electrostatic force.

Introduce Science Experiment

1. Ask students if they remember what a force is.
   - Grade 1: If nobody remembers, remind them that it is a push or a pull. Talk about how magnets, gravity, elastics, your muscles, and other forces move things.
   - Grades 2 and 3: Ask students if they remember some of the forces you talked about in Language.
2. Ask students if they think all forces move all objects.

Science Experiment

See page 70 for the Primary Science Experiment sheet.

1. Hand out the Primary Science Experiment sheet (page 70) and ask students to write their name on it.
2. Show students how the experiment will be done.
   - Grades 1 and 2: Show students the magnet and elastic and how they are able to move things. Explain that to use gravity, they should drop each object. For muscular force, they can pick the object up. Show students the objects they will try to move.
   - Grade 3: Ask the students to take out their ruler. Read the instructions together. Ask students how they will use a magnet to move an object. How will they use an elastic? Continue with each force, making sure students know how to use each force: e.g., to use gravity, they should drop each object; for muscular force,, they can pick the object up.

Be sure to mention that objects should not go flying across the room when students use the elastics but only travel a short distance over the desktop.

Remind students that the elastics are not for playing.

3. Show students how to record their findings.
   - Grade 1: Do all the boxes for the paper clip together as a class, showing them how to put a check if it moves and an X if it doesn't move.
   - Grade 2: Do two or three of the boxes for the paper clip together as a class, showing them how to put a check if it moves and an X if it doesn't move.
   - Grade 3: Ask students to use their rulers to measure how far each object moves. If they are unable to measure it with their ruler, they can simply put an X if it did not move and a check if it did move.
4. Divide the students into groups of four. Give each group the objects they need. Monitor groups carefully to make sure no one is using the elastics as projectiles.
   - Grade 1: If groups are having trouble, consider doing the whole experiment as a class.
5. Color a picture of the experiment when finished.

Take Up Science Experiment

Ask students if their muscles could move all the objects. Ask students if gravity could move all the objects. Ask if a magnet could move all the objects. Discuss why the magnet can't move all the objects.
- Grade 1: Continue with the other forces.
- Grade 2: Ask students if they can think of other forces that were not in the experiment.
- Grade 3: Ask which forces could be measured with a ruler (magnet and elastic) and which forces could not be measured with a ruler (muscular force and gravity).

Get Ready for Recess

Remind students to take their snack and all their clothing: coats, outdoor shoes, etc.

- Grade 1: Yes, you really do have to remind them every time!
- Grades 2 and 3: If it has warmed up during the afternoon, they may not need their coats.

Period 4: Art: Draw a Superhero

Introduce Art Activity

Ask students if they remember some of the things that made objects move in the Science Experiment: e.g., magnets, gravity, elastics. Ask students to think of ways these forces could help superheroes move: e.g., a huge elastic could help a superhero fly.

Art Activity

1. Hand out blank pieces of paper and ask students to write their name on them.
2. Ask students to draw something that would help a superhero move. Tell them that their pictures should be big; i.e., we can see it and it looks close. Remind students to draw things in the background (e.g., houses or other people) smaller so they look far away.
   - Grades 2 and 3: Ask students to do their best, neat work and not to rush to finish.
3. Students will probably finish this quickly, so ask them to add more detail to their pictures; e.g., more color, more things in the background. You may be able to find some things they can glue onto their picture: e.g., bits of yarn for hair or beads for eyes, etc. You can also glue their drawings on construction paper and ask students to draw patterns on the construction paper frames. Students can draw a second picture if they like.
   - If there is still time, play an extra game (see page 58) or give some free time.

Clean Up Classroom/Get Ready to Go Home

It always takes a while to clean up after Art. I ask every student to pick up five or ten things from the floor to make sure the floor is clean and all the art supplies are back where they belong. Ask students to put their chairs up on their desk and get their coats and backpacks. Make sure they do not forget their lunch bags. In some classes, children have specific jobs at the end of the day, such as closing the blinds and erasing the boards. Dismiss each student to an adult. Any child who has not been picked up after 5 or 10 minutes can be taken to the office to wait for their parent/guardian there.

Extra Activities and Games

It may be that you find you have some extra time. Or students may simply need a break and it's time for an activity or game.

Grade 1

Singing

Sing the alphabet and students stand up when you get to the first letter of their names—or any letter of their name. Sing nursery rhymes or a song they know, or you can teach them a song. Sing "Row, Row, Row Your Boat" normally, then quietly, then in an opera voice, then as if you are sad, etc.

Doggy, Doggy, Who's Got Your Bone?

This game is played with students sitting in a circle or at their desks. One student has a pencil. One student in the middle of the circle or at the front of the class is the Doggy. Everyone closes their eyes and puts their hands behind their backs except for the student with the pencil. Everyone chants

> Doggy, Doggy, who's got your bone?
> Somebody stole it from your home.
> Guess who? Maybe you.
> Maybe the monkey from the Zoo.
> Wake up, Doggy. Find your bone.
> If you find it, bring it home.

While everyone (or maybe only you the first couple of times) says the rhyme, the student with the pencil walks around and puts it in the hands of another student and then goes back to their place. When the rhyme is done, everyone opens their eyes and the Doggy takes up to three guesses as to who has the pencil. Other students take turns being the Doggy or the person with the pencil.

Sleeping Beauty

I love this game. All adults love this game! Students put their heads down on their desks or lie down on the carpet. The object of the game is not to move. When you see a student move, you call them and they sit up. They can help look for students who are moving but they are not allowed to touch anyone. The game continues until one sleeping beauty is left.

Grade 2

I often use the promise of fun and games for the last 15 minutes of class as an incentive for finishing work or being quiet.

Singing

Grade 2 students really like to sing. You probably already know many songs that they know. You can ask what they would like to sing; when they get to a song you know, sing it.

Murder Monster

Everyone closes their eyes. Touch one student on the top of the head; this is the Murder Monster. Students open their eyes and walk around the room randomly. The Murder Monster winks or blinks at people. People who have been winked (or blinked) at must pretend to die (preferably a loud and glorious death). Anyone may guess who the Murder Monster is by putting up their hand. If the guesser is wrong, he or she must pretend to die. Students up to Grade 5 or 6 love this game.

Bip/Bop

Students stand in a circle or at their desks. You have a ball, an eraser, or a crumpled piece of paper. You say "Bip" and throw the ball to one student. The student catches it, says "Bop," and throws it back to you. If the student misses the ball or doesn't say "Bop," he/she has to sit down. Continue throwing the ball to students faster and faster until only one student is left standing.

Grade 3

The incentive of games or free time at the end of the day really helps Grade 3 students do their best work quietly. You can play Hangman using the words from the lesson that day. Grade 3 students love playing Simon Says as long as you make it a bit tricky to get them out; they also love being Simon and getting other students out.

Ball/Name Game

Students stand in a circle or around the edge of the classroom with balls/erasers/crumpled paper. Students say the name of the person they are throwing to. If they say the wrong name, drop the ball, or throw badly, they sit down. Continue until only one person is standing.

A alternative way to play: the first time students miss the ball, they can get the letter *B* and stay standing; the second time they miss, they get the letter *O*; the third time, the letter *P*. This way they have three tries before they sit down. Choose longer words to spell if you don't want anyone to sit down.

An alternative way to play: When students first miss the ball, they get the letter *O* and stay standing; the second time they miss, they get the letter *U*; the third time, the letter *T*. This way they have three tries before they sit down. Choose longer words to spell if you don't want anyone to sit down.

Primary Cloze Activity: Super Student Learns about Forces

Name: _____ Date: _____

Fill in the blanks using these words:

force, gravity, magnet, muscular force, friction, electrostatic force, push, pull, speed, load, distance

1. Super Student thinks he/she is a force but really a force is a *push* or a ☐☐☐☐.

2. Super Student chased Super Villain, who was carrying a ☐☐☐☐ of stolen school pencils.

3. Super Student thought he/she could use ☐☐☐☐☐☐☐☐☐☐☐☐☐ to jump over the principal and catch Super Villain.

4. Unfortunately, the force of ☐☐☐☐☐☐☐ caused Super Student to fall on the principal.

5. Next, Super Villain ran into the library and over the carpet with only socks on, so that when Super Student caught up, Super Villain could use

   ☐☐☐☐☐☐☐☐☐☐☐☐☐☐☐☐☐ to shock our hero!

6. As Super Villain ran past the office, the principal used a really big ☐☐☐☐☐☐

   to pull Super Villain back toward the office. (Everyone knows Super Villain wears iron underwear!)

7. Super Villain tried to use the ☐☐☐☐☐☐☐☐ between his/her shoes and the floor to stop, but the shoes were in the library and the socks were slippery!

8. Super Villain was sliding toward the principal and gaining ☐☐☐☐☐, so Super Student pushed the principal out of the way!

9. Super Villain crashed into Super Student, and Super Villain, Super Student, the principal, and the pencils flew a great ☐☐☐☐☐☐☐☐ in every direction.

10. "Super Student," said the principal, "you are a ☐☐☐☐☐. You and Super Villain have detention."

Pembroke Publishers ©2016 *Substitute Teaching?* by Amanda Yuill ISBN 978-1-55138-312-5

Answer Key for Primary Cloze Activity: Super Student Learns about Forces

1. Super Student thinks he/she is a force but really a force is a <u>push</u> or a <u>pull</u>.
2. Super Student chased Super Villain who was carrying a <u>load</u> of stolen school pencils.
3. Super Student thought he/she could use <u>muscular force</u> to jump over the principal and catch Super Villain.
4. Unfortunately, the force of <u>gravity</u> caused Super Student to fall on the principal.
5. Next, Super Villain ran into the library and over the carpet with only socks on so that when Super Student caught up, he could use <u>electrostatic force</u> to shock our hero!
6. As Super Villain ran past the office, the principal used a really big <u>magnet</u> to pull Super Villain back toward the office. (Everyone knows Super Villain wears iron underwear!)
7. Super Villain tried to use the <u>friction</u> between his/her shoes and the floor to stop but the shoes were in the library and the socks were slippery!
8. As Super Villain slid towards the principal, he/she was gaining <u>speed,</u> so Super Student pushed the principal out of the way!
9. Super Villain crashed into Super Student, and Super Villain, Super Student, the principal, and the pencils flew a great <u>distance</u> in every direction.
10. "Super Student," said the principal, "you are a <u>force</u>. You and Super Villain have detention."

Pembroke Publishers ©2016 *Substitute Teaching?* by Amanda Yuill ISBN 978-1-55138-312-5

Primary Language Activity

Name: _____   Date: _____

Word List

force	friction	speed
gravity	electrostatic force	load
magnet	push	distance
muscular force	pull	

1. Put the words in ABC (alphabetical) order.

_____

_____

2. Use each word in a sentence.

_____

_____

_____

_____

_____

_____

_____

_____

_____

_____

_____

_____

3. Draw a picture of each word. Use the back of this page if you need more space.

Pembroke Publishers ©2016 *Substitute Teaching?* by Amanda Yuill ISBN 978-1-55138-312-5

Primary Writing Activity

Name: _____ Date: _____

If you were a superhero that had super powers with one kind of force, which force would it be and what would your superpower be? What would you do with your super powers? Draw a picture.

_____

_____

_____

_____

_____

_____

_____

_____

Pembroke Publishers ©2016 *Substitute Teaching?* by Amanda Yuill ISBN 978-1-55138-312-5

Extra Language Activity: Primary Word Search

Name: _____   Date : _____

P	U	S	H	C	J	I	P	Q	U	P	C	G	Q	H
I	M	J	L	R	K	R	L	W	M	E	N	H	O	I
B	S	P	E	E	D	Q	U	Z	A	P	O	R	F	S
A	B	Q	U	A	O	T	M	A	G	N	E	T	Y	H
R	Z	L	U	Q	I	V	Y	P	W	B	V	G	F	P
V	Y	H	R	A	S	V	M	Q	G	W	L	O	A	D
W	A	Y	X	S	I	G	E	Z	W	J	D	Y	E	J
E	L	E	C	T	R	O	S	T	A	T	I	C	G	T
Z	U	A	K	Z	O	F	E	X	F	D	C	X	V	D
K	B	Y	J	M	U	S	C	U	L	A	R	N	C	F
A	D	D	X	U	L	K	F	R	I	C	T	I	O	N
T	C	R	D	E	X	C	S	K	X	M	M	N	G	L
J	N	J	T	G	T	Z	F	H	N	V	D	E	B	E
H	I	S	T	B	D	I	S	T	A	N	C	E	M	O
F	O	R	C	E	H	B	W	S	C	N	I	L	F	K

Find These Words

PUSH   ELECTROSTATIC   FRICTION
SPEED   MUSCULAR   LOAD
DISTANCE   FORCE   MAGNET

Pembroke Publishers ©2016 *Substitute Teaching?* by Amanda Yuill ISBN 978-1-55138-312-5

Answer Key for Primary Word Search

P	U	S	H										
	S	P	E	E	D								
							M	A	G	N	E	T	
										L	O	A	D
E	L	E	C	T	R	O	S	T	A	T	I	C	
				M	U	S	C	U	L	A	R		
							F	R	I	C	T	I	O	N
					D	I	S	T	A	N	C	E	
F	O	R	C	E									

Extra Language Activity: Primary Crossword

Name: _____   Date: _____

Word List

friction   distance
magnet   mass
speed   muscular
electrostatic gravity
push   force
pull

Across

2. moving quickly
4. the force that causes things to fall
5. a push or a pull
6. the force that causes shocks
7. a piece of iron or steel that attracts certain objects
8. to press against something

Down

1. the amount of space between two things
3. the force caused by using your muscles
5. the force caused by two things rubbing against each other
7. the weight of an object
8. to draw something towards

Pembroke Publishers ©2016 *Substitute Teaching?* by Amanda Yuill ISBN 978-1-55138-312-5

Primary Math Sheet

1. Add. Use counters if needed.

1	4	5	8	7	2	3	6	9	4
+3	+2	+3	+1	+2	+6	+3	+1	+1	+4

9	5	3	4	7	5	2	6	8	1
+2	+5	+8	+8	+5	+7	+8	+6	+4	+9

2. Finish the pattern by coloring in the boxes.

1	2	3	4	5	6	7	8	9	10
11	12	13	14	15	16	17	18	19	20
21	22	23	24	25	26	27	28	29	30
31	32	33	34	35	36	37	38	39	40
41	42	43	44	45	46	47	48	49	50
51	52	53	54	55	56	57	58	59	60
61	62	63	64	65	66	67	68	69	70
71	72	73	74	75	76	77	78	79	80
81	82	83	84	85	86	87	88	89	90
91	92	93	94	95	96	97	98	99	100

1	2	3	4	5	6	7	8	9	10
11	12	13	14	15	16	17	18	19	20
21	22	23	24	25	26	27	28	29	30
31	32	33	34	35	36	37	38	39	40
41	42	43	44	45	46	47	48	49	50
51	52	53	54	55	56	57	58	59	60
61	62	63	64	65	66	67	68	69	70
71	72	73	74	75	76	77	78	79	80
81	82	83	84	85	86	87	88	89	90
91	92	93	94	95	96	97	98	99	100

3. Ask your friends their favorite color and make a graph.

Favorite Colors in the Class

6								
5								
4								
3								
2								
1								
	Blue	Red	Yellow	Green	Purple	Pink	Orange	Other

Pembroke Publishers ©2016 *Substitute Teaching?* by Amanda Yuill ISBN 978-1-55138-312-5

Primary Math Sheet (continued)

4. Add. Use counters if needed.

11	42	35	48	57	62	73	86	88	94
+83	+82	+63	+51	+42	+36	+2	+1	+1	+4

97	58	37	46	75	65	42	32	82	10
+22	+51	+82	+83	+54	+73	+8	+6	+4	+9

5. Complete the patterns.

10, 20, 30, _____, _____, _____, _____, _____, _____, _____

3, 6, 9, _____, _____, _____, _____, _____, _____, _____

100, 200, 300, _____, _____, _____, _____, _____, _____

50, 100, 150, 200, _____, _____, _____, _____, _____

100, 90, 80, _____, _____, _____, _____, _____, _____, _____

6. Subtract. Use counters if needed.

10	4	5	8	7	8	3	6	9	4
−3	−2	−3	−1	−2	−6	−3	−1	−1	−4

9	5	10	9	7	10	9	6	8	10
−2	−5	−8	−8	−5	−7	−8	−6	−4	−9

7. Maya had 5 cats. A friend gave her 8 more cats. How many cats did Maya have all together?

8. Maya had 10 cats. She gave 3 cats to her friend. How many cats did Maya have left?

9. Maya had 3 cats. Each cat had 5 kittens. How many kittens did Maya have all together?

Pembroke Publishers ©2016 *Substitute Teaching?* by Amanda Yuill ISBN 978-1-55138-312-5

Answer Key for Primary Math Sheet

1.

1	4	5	8	7	2	3	6	9	4
+3	+2	+3	+1	+2	+6	+3	+1	+1	+4
4	6	8	9	9	8	6	7	10	8

9	5	3	4	7	5	2	6	8	1
+2	+5	+8	+8	+5	+7	+8	+6	+4	+9
11	10	11	12	12	12	10	12	12	10

2.

1	2	3	4	5	6	7	8	9	10
11	12	13	14	15	16	17	18	19	20
21	22	23	24	25	26	27	28	29	30
31	32	33	34	35	36	37	38	39	40
41	42	43	44	45	46	47	48	49	50
51	52	53	54	55	56	57	58	59	60
61	62	63	64	65	66	67	68	69	70
71	72	73	74	75	76	77	78	79	80
81	82	83	84	85	86	87	88	89	90
91	92	93	94	95	96	97	98	99	100

1	2	3	4	5	6	7	8	9	10
11	12	13	14	15	16	17	18	19	20
21	22	23	24	25	26	27	28	29	30
31	32	33	34	35	36	37	38	39	40
41	42	43	44	45	46	47	48	49	50
51	52	53	54	55	56	57	58	59	60
61	62	63	64	65	66	67	68	69	70
71	72	73	74	75	76	77	78	79	80
81	82	83	84	85	86	87	88	89	90
91	92	93	94	95	96	97	98	99	100

3. Answers will vary

4.

11	42	35	48	57	62	73	86	88	94
+83	+82	+63	+51	+42	+36	+2	+1	+1	+4
94	124	98	99	99	98	75	87	89	98

97	58	37	46	75	65	42	32	82	10
+22	+51	+82	+83	+54	+73	+8	+6	+4	+9
119	109	119	129	129	138	50	38	86	19

5. 10, 20, 30, 40, 50, 60, 70, 80, 90, 100
   3, 6, 9, 12, 15, 18, 21, 24, 27, 30
   100, 200, 300, 400, 500, 600, 700, 800, 900
   50, 100, 150, 200, 250, 300, 350, 400, 450
   100, 90, 80, 70, 60, 50, 40, 30, 20, 10

6.

10	4	5	8	7	8	3	6	9	4
−3	−2	−3	−1	−2	−6	−3	−1	−1	−4
7	2	2	7	5	2	0	5	8	0

9	5	10	9	7	10	9	6	8	10
−2	−5	−8	−8	−5	−7	−8	−6	−4	−9
7	0	2	1	2	3	1	0	4	1

7. 5 + 8 = 13 Maya had 13 cats altogether
8. 10 − 3 = 7 Maya had 7 cats left.
9. 3 x 5 = 15 or 5 + 5 + 5 = 15 Maya had 15 kittens altogether.

Pembroke Publishers ©2016 *Substitute Teaching?* by Amanda Yuill ISBN 978-1-55138-312-5

Primary Science Experiment: Forces

Name: _____   Date: _____

Try to move many different objects with many different forces. Measure how far the object moves. If you can't measure it, put a check if it did move and an X if it didn't move.

Force ⇓

Magnet					
Elastic					
Gravity					
Muscle					
Other					
Object ⇒	Paper clip	Eraser	Pencil	Paper	Other

1. Did all of the forces move all of the objects? Why do you think that is?

_____

_____

_____

_____

_____

_____

_____

_____

5

Substitute Teaching Junior Grades

Grade 4: They Can Finally Tie Their Shoelaces

I was teaching a Grade 4 class for a week while the principal was looking for someone to cover the second half of a maternity leave. We were in a portable. One afternoon, one of the boys in the class was very upset about something that had happened at recess and ran out of the portable before I could stop him. One of his friends said, "I'll get him," and ran out of the portable too! Before I could respond to that, one of the other boys saw that this wasn't okay; he told me, "I'll go tell them to come back" and ran out too. I moved to the door as fast as I could and stood in front of it before I was the only one left in the portable!!

What Grade 4 Students Are Like

Physically

By Grade 4, students are not having accidents anymore and they usually can make it to the bathroom if they are going to be sick. They are able to tie their shoelaces and put on their winter clothes by themselves. Sometimes they will still need help with stuck zippers; however, another student is likely to be able to help them.

In a typical Grade 4 class, the children have not entered puberty, except for a couple of the girls. As in Grade 3, most boys do not know how to handle this. It's good to let them know if they are saying something inappropriate without coming down too hard on them, as they really don't know yet what is okay and what is not.

In the junior grades, children are more likely to feel pressure to get good grades than when they were in primary classes. Some students will have stomach aches when they are anxious or worried, especially about a test or assignment that is due. When children complain of a stomach ache, have them get a drink of water and use the bathroom and come back. If I know they have a test that day, ask them if they feel ready for the test. Sometimes just talking about it will make them feel better. Of course, sometimes a stomach ache just means they need to go to the bathroom.

Socially

Students don't want to be known as a tattle-tale or snitch. This means that they will often bear bad behavior instead of telling the teacher and getting help. Friendship is more important to them than how they are treated. I sometimes remind a class that it is okay to tell on someone who is hurting you and doesn't stop when you tell them to stop, or who doesn't apologize when they have hurt you.

Belonging to a group of friends or at least having one good friend to share things with is very important. One way girls in Grade 4 show their friendship is by passing notes to each other in class. In order to discourage this, I sometimes take the note and pretend to read it out loud. However, instead of reading what the note really says, I make up ridiculous things. I go on so long that everyone knows the note could not say that much. For example, I may "read" the following:

> Dear Sally, how are you today? I am good except for all that ice cream I ate last night—it's giving me gas today. Doesn't Billy look handsome today? I just love what he's done with his hair. Do you want to come over and watch TV after school? We could watch (list shows) and have snacks like (list snacks).

In primary classes, students still try to solve their problems physically—by pushing people that push them and hitting people who call them names. By Grade 4, students are trying to solve their problems verbally. This is still challenging for them and they may need support and help to do this well.

Academically

Diary of a Wimpy Kid, *Amulet* (a graphic novel), *Charlotte's Web*, and *Because of Mr. Terupt* are all books that students in Grade 4 enjoy reading. Grade 4 students are able to understand the main idea when they read and to give a summary, including the main idea, characters, setting, the main problem, and how it was solved.

By Grade 4, students know how to write a paragraph and are able to add detail—especially sensory details—to simple sentences. Students are able to write for 20 minutes without interruption or getting up (to use the electric pencil sharpener, for example).

Grade 4 students have been introduced to multiplication; however, many are still memorizing basic multiplication facts. Students are still learning how to divide and may have some difficulty with dividing larger numbers. Adding and subtracting triple digits, telling time, and measuring should all be easy review by Grade 4. Students are introduced to decimals to the tenth and adding and subtracting fractions.

How to Teach Grade 4 Well

Grade 4 students will need to move around about every 40 minutes. This often corresponds with the periods in Grade 4; aim to have them move a bit in between every period. If students are getting antsy in the middle of a period, sometimes it is a good idea to have a small break to play a quick game of Simon Says or do jumping jacks before going on with the lesson.

Grade 4 students are becoming more independent in their problem-solving. Primary students will tell you that they lost their pencil, whereas Grade 4 students will look for it a bit before coming to tell you they lost their pencil. It is good to encourage students to try to find their own solutions to problems; for example, asking to borrow a pencil from a friend.

Grade 4 students usually play and hang out with their own gender. When putting students into pairs for an activity, pairing them with a member of the opposite sex might cause some students to sigh loudly. It is always good to remind students to treat others the way that they would like to be treated—even if they are paired with a girl!

Musically, Grade 4 students are in between being small children who still like Disney and pre-teens who enjoy rap songs. Grade 4 children will like it all, even if they don't quite understand what the lyrics are saying. Sometimes this leads to students talking about inappropriate things because they don't understand what they are saying. It's good to keep this in mind so that the consequences for saying something inappropriate match the crime that wasn't really intended!

Grade 5: They're So Nice

A friend of mine was engaged. She was teaching Grade 5. One of the girls asked if she was married. My friend said not yet, but she was going to get married soon. A while later, the same student asked if she was married yet. My friend responded that she was not married yet. The student asked her how long it took to get married!

What Grade 5 Students Are Like

Physically

As in Grades 3 and 4, some of the girls are starting puberty. They are much more conscious of their bodies and sensitive to remarks. While younger students brush off comments quite easily, Grade 5 girls are more likely to take them to heart and be hurt. It is good to foster a respectful atmosphere and quickly stop any unkind comments. It may be necessary to explain that, although a comment might sound neutral to the speaker, it can hurt another student; if that is the case, it is good to apologize and say that you didn't intend to hurt anyone. This may cause rolling of eyes in the speaker, who thinks the other student is too sensitive, but it is good practice in empathy.

Some Grade 5 students have started to grow and others have not. The girls tend to have done more of their growing than the boys, leading to a lot of the girls being taller than the boys. The tall students are also very excited if they are nearing the teacher's height. They enjoy seeing if they are close to being taller than the teacher.

Every now and then Grade 5 students will have growing pains. This happens in all grades, with increasing frequency as they move toward puberty and growth spurts. It is especially common for kids to have growing pains in the arms and legs. If students complain that their arms or legs hurt, make sure they didn't injure themselves at recess or another time. If they haven't, tell students that it's probably a growing pain and that it will go away in a couple of minutes; if it doesn't, they can tell their parents when they get home. If students continue to complain, I send them to the office to get ice. Ice is magic in elementary school—it not only cures swelling but any number of ailments, such as growing pains, headaches, ingrown toenails, and bad marks.

Socially

A lot of Grade 5 kids want to help. It is in their blood to help teachers, smaller children, and animals. If you just let them help you out, you would make their life worth living. The great thing about this is that they are actually helpful. Collating papers, cleaning blackboards, preparing art lessons, washing your car—they will do it all! Of course, it isn't always done as well as you would have done it but, hey, it's done—even if sometimes page 7 comes before page 5.

Grade 5 students are blissfully independent without the attitude. It is really a nice grade to teach. They still want to please you and have your approval. When you say, "Please take out your books and read," Grade 5 students know where their books are, know where to find a book if they don't have a book, take their books out, and start reading. Of course, they are not perfect, so you may have to give a reminder or two to not chat or to help a student pick a book out of the class library. But mostly Grade 5 classes are so nice!

In Grade 5, girls are still mostly friends with girls, and boys are friends with boys. The girls become more and more chatty. They make up dance or gymnastic routines and talk about movies, TV shows, and the latest boy bands. The boys play soccer, basketball, and video games, and talk about cars and TV shows. Of course, this is an over-generalization—but stereotypes have to come from somewhere!

Academically

A Wrinkle in Time, *The Hobbit*, and *Wonder* are books students enjoy reading in Grade 5. Grade 5 students also enjoy books based on movies and graphic novels. Besides being able to identify the plot, characters, and setting in what they read, Grade 5 students can place themselves in a character's place and say what they would have done differently in that situation. They are able to give their opinion on the book, saying if they would recommend it to someone else and why.

Using more complex sentences with conjunctions and details, Grade 5 students can write a few paragraphs in a row in one sitting. They are able to state a point of view and give reasons for it. They are able to state the main idea of a book or lesson and give supporting evidence. They are able to proofread, revise, and improve their writing and use drafts before submitting a final copy.

Multiplication and division facts are memorized by Grade 5 and students are learning to do long division. They can multiply two-digit numbers by two-digit numbers and divide three-digit numbers by one-digit numbers. Students know numbers up to 100,000 and down to 0.01. They are able to compare fractions and convert fractions to decimals.

How to Teach Grade 5 Well

Their sense of humor is maturing and developing, so Grade 5 students are starting to understand sarcasm. However, they still laugh when a friend falls over or farts loudly (to be honest, I know a few grown men who still find this funny). They are still learning political correctness, so some of their jokes are a bit off-color because they simply don't have the sophistication to know what's not appropriate. Grade 5 students still like riddles.

Like older students, Grade 5 students will enjoy it if you know something about pop culture—the latest boy bands or the video games. The pop culture they like is still aimed at children and not the pop culture of adults. Most adults, therefore, don't know anything about it, so the kids are very impressed if you can come out with the name of a band and a song, or know something about how to get past a certain level in a popular video game.

Grade 5 students should be able to sit through an entire lesson without needing to move around. However, I often teach a lesson and then allow for some movement as students get their textbooks or come to take a sheet of paper. If there is a choice between someone handing out papers and students coming to get them, I sometimes allow students to come and get the paper just so they have a chance to move.

Grade 5 students really enjoy working toward a goal and seeing the rewards of that. Incentives work very well and students often encourage each other to sit quietly so that they can get the promised free time or game. They will love you if you end the day with a game or free time. I really like playing games with Grade 5 students because they have fun and really get into it.

Grade 6: Spring Fever!

I was teaching a Grade 6 class when they were given a presentation from the police. An officer was telling students what happens when someone gets arrested and goes to jail. He had a display of contraband taken from prisoners, basically knives made from anything and everything, including a toothbrush and soap. He talked about the cavity check and went on to describe how the showers and toilets had no doors on the stalls. At this point the boy who was sitting beside me (to help him remember to listen politely instead of chatting with his friends) said, "Jail sucks, man!"

What Grade 6 Students Are Like

Physically

Grade 6 students can stink and not know it, or not care. In fact, it is a well-known fact that often the only way a Grade 6 boy will start wearing deodorant is if he likes a girl. Ditto for taking showers and wearing clean underwear every day. You may want to open the windows and air out the classroom at lunch, even in the cold weather.

As students enter puberty, they have increased strength and physical abilities. This is the time where many students show a real aptitude for sports and it becomes more important in their lives. Perhaps you have been at a Grade 6 house-league floor hockey game where the outcome is a life-or-death affair, with proportional determination and reactions from the players in the form of a lot of pushing and shoving and swearing under their breath.

Speaking of pushing and shoving, puberty also causes students to be moody sometimes. (Insert sarcastic laugh of mothers with pre-teen kids here.) It can also lead to outbursts of anger for seemingly unimportant things, leading to more pushing and shoving. Sometimes it's really hard to tell if the boys are just fooling around or if they are seriously angry—sometimes they don't know themselves. Of course, to get out of trouble they always say they were just fooling around!

Socially

Ah, spring fever! It sometimes erupts in Grade 4 or 5; however, it is definitely contagious in Grade 6! Somes girls might giggle and draw hearts on their homework. Some boys bother, pester, and basically torment the objects of their desire. There's nothing like reading test answers with little hearts as the dots over the *is* and asking Johnny to stop taking Susie's pencil crayons and hiding them for the hundredth time. Should I just tell him that it's not his name with little hearts all around it on the inside of her binder and put him out of his misery? Maybe not…

Grade 6 students are starting to believe that maybe they do not have to please the teacher, that perhaps their friends' approval is more important than the teacher's approval. Mostly they are just starting to consider this idea. They can still usually be won over with a few stories and incentives, for which they decide that they do want your approval after all. They try to act cool, like they don't care what you say, but they are easily found out when they get excited about the games you introduce.

Friends' opinions are more and more important, so peer pressure becomes more of an issue for Grade 6 students. They desperately want to fit in and to be liked, and are more susceptible to negative peer pressure than when they were younger and the teacher's approval mattered more. This is aggravated by their gradual understanding that their parents and teachers do not, in fact, know everything, and that they may even be wrong sometimes. Even students who normally are the picture of responsibility can be led down the garden path every now and then by peer pressure and convinced to, say, moon people out the window.

Academically

Tuck Everlasting, *The Secret Garden*, and the Harry Potter books are all books commonly read in Grade 6. Grade 6 students can understand increasingly complex texts and are able to understand not only the main idea of the book but also the moral or point that the author is trying to make. Students are able to express whether they agree with the author's viewpoint and give reasons for their opinions.

Grade 6 students can gather information, make an outline, write an assignment, edit it, and write the final copy fairly independently or with some help from the teacher. They are able to decide which information they have gathered is relevant to their assignment. They can use supporting evidence to make their point. Of course, in every class there is a wide variety of skills and abilities; therefore, some students will need more help than others.

Numbers up to 1,000,000 and down to 0.001 are commonly used in Grade 6; students are expected to understand and use these numbers properly. But students sometimes still have trouble knowing how to read out numbers over 100,000. Students are able to use mixed numbers like 1½ and improper fractions like 5/4, and are able to represent a mixed number as an improper fraction and vice versa. Students are using multiplication and division in multi-step word problems.

How to Teach Grade 6 Well

By Grade 6, students are expected to sit for a whole period and concentrate on their work without needing to move around or becoming restless. It is still good to give a bit of time between periods for students to get up, move around, and talk a bit, but no more than five minutes are needed. This, of course, depends on the class. There are always those classes who need more movement than a whole herd of Grade 1 students.

Grade 6 students have quite an advanced sense of humor; they are able to joke with you and even surprise you with some good lines relevant to the topic being discussed. They still enjoy riddles and pun-based jokes; e.g., Why didn't the skeleton cross the road? Because he had no guts.

Grade 6 students really enjoy free time and it can be used as an incentive to finish work and ensure proper behavior. You will find that they are less likely to choose activity-based play during free time than younger ones. Students may simply talk with friends or play a card game. Some students will be content to sit and read.

By Grade 6, students are becoming more and more socially aware. They will want to discuss world events they have heard about on the news or social justice issues. If there is time, it is good to give 5 or 10 minutes to talk about these issues if they come up in the course of a lesson, and to encourage students to be empathetic while considering all points of view.

Junior Day Plan and Lessons

Junior Day Plan: Airplanes

Starting Routines
  Self-Introduction/Attendance/Joke, Story, Fact, etc.: 10 minutes
  Silent reading: 15 minutes
Period 1: Language
  Introduce Cloze Activity and Language Activity: 5 minutes
  Cloze and Language Activities: 20 minutes
  Introduce Writing Activity: 5 minutes
  Writing Activity: 15 minutes
  * Optional: Students who finish early can do extra language activities; these activities can be used at any time students are finished work early during the day.
Get Ready for Recess: 5 minutes; 10 minutes in winter.
Recess
Period 2: Math
  Math Game: 15 minutes
  Introduce Math Sheet: 5 minutes
  Math Sheet: 40 minutes
  Take Up Math Sheet: 10 minutes
Get Ready for Lunch: 5 minutes
Lunch
Afternoon Routines
  Attendance/Joke, Story, Fact, etc.: 10 minutes
Period 3: Science
  Introduce Science Experiment: 10 minutes
  Science Experiment: 40 minutes
  Take Up Science Experiment: 10 minutes
Get Ready for Recess: 5 minutes; 10 minutes in winter
Recess
Period 4: Art
  Introduce Art Activity: 10 minutes
  Art Activity: 50 minutes
Clean Up Classroom/Get Ready to Go Home: 15 minutes
Home Time

Starting Routines

Self-Introduction/Attendance/Joke, Story, Fact, etc.

- Grade 4: Students still like the silly things that primary students like, even though they are trying to grow out of them. Slapstick and toilet humor will still get big laughs. Knock-knock jokes and riddles are also a good way to go.
- Grade 5: I like to tell the story of Mt. Pelée, a volcano on the French island of Martinique that erupted in 1902, killing around 30,000 people. They were killed by a fast-moving cloud of hot gas and rocks. Only three people survived: a man on the edge of town who had severe burns all over his body; a little girl who took a boat to a cave and was found hours later, unconscious in her boat; and a man who had been put in a dungeon because he had been in a fight the night before.
- Grade 6: Grade 6 students will be impressed if you watch a popular TV show and can talk about what happened in the latest episode, or if you know something about a couple of popular bands, such as an upcoming concert. For those of you who, like me, lack any knowledge of pop culture, you can still be cool if you know trivia about your city or town that includes a ghost story!

Silent Reading

Students will have a book they are reading in their desk or backpack. There are usually many books in the classroom that the students can read if they do not. If the class is reading a book together, read the next chapter. I try to use different voices for each character and make it really interesting.

- Grade 5: One student could read their book to the class.
- Grade 6: Ask students if anyone is reading a good book and if they would like to read from it. Have a few students tell why they like the book they are reading right now, give a short summary of the plot (with no spoilers), and read the first couple of pages or a part of the book they really like.

Period 1: Language

Introduce Cloze Activity

- Grade 4: Ask if students know what *accident-prone* means. Talk about the sorts of things that could happen to someone who is accident-prone. Ask if they have ever had a day when they kept hurting themselves. We all have those days when we stub our toe and then drop our bag on it—the same toe, of course, the same toe!
- Grade 5: Ask students how many parts of an airplane they can name. Draw an airplane on the board and invite students to come up and label parts of it. Or project the airplane graphic on page 79 on the interactive whiteboard with the labels deleted.
- Grade 6: Ask students to raise their hands if they would like to jump out of an airplane with a parachute. Ask why or why not.

If this is too difficult, draw the inside of an airplane and ask them to label things found there; e.g., seats, bathrooms, cockpit, etc.

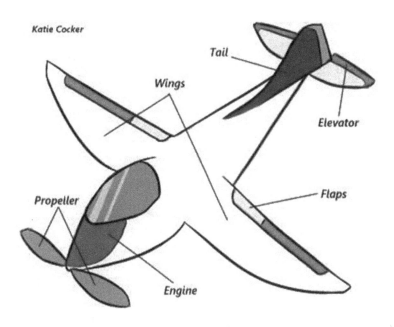

Katie Cocker

Tail

Wings

Elevator

Flaps

Propeller

Engine

Cloze Activity

See page 88 for the Junior Cloze Activity sheet; page 89 for the Answer Key for Junior Cloze Activity.

1. Hand out the Junior Cloze Activity sheet (page 88). Ask students to write their name on it. Read over the list of words with the class.
   - Grade 6: Ask if they know the meaning of any of the words.
2. Ask students if they know the following kinds of planes: a prop plane (a plane with a propeller), a jet (a very fast plane), and a glider (a plane without an engine).
3. Ask if students know any parts of a plane from the list: propeller (the blades on the nose of a plane); engine (the part of the airplane that uses gas to make the plane go); wings (the two long arms of a plane); flaps (the parts of the wings that go up and down and make the plane go up and down); tail (the back part that stabilizes the plane); elevator (the part that looks like flaps at the back that makes the plane turn).
   - Grade 5: If there are any parts of a plane on the list that students did not mention during the introduction, ask if they can guess what parts of the plane they are and what they do.
4. Ask students if they can think of anything that would help a plane fly or hinder a plane from flying: e.g., drag (the force of air against the plane), thrust (forward force), lift (upward force), weight (the heaviness of something or downward force). You might want to write a few of the more difficult terms or terms the students are not familiar with on the board.
5. Ask students if they know what *aerodynamics* means (the flow of air around an object).
6. Have students complete the Cloze Activity. Collect the sheets for the teacher and leave with the answer key (page 89).

Introduce Language Activity

- Grade 4: Ask students to raise their hands if they have ever been on an airplane. Ask if they have ever been on a prop plane or a jet or a glider. If they could choose between the three types of planes, which type of plane would they like to ride in?
- Grade 5: Ask students how they think a glider gets off the ground if it has no engine (it is towed up by a prop plane). Ask: *How does a glider fly with*

no engine? (It relies on air flow and the design of the wings to keep them in the air.) Ask how they think a glider lands (the pilot returns the glider to the runway and uses the part of the glider called a spoiler to slow it down and land).

- Grade 6: Ask students if they have ever seen an airshow. Have they ever heard an airplane after it has flown by? Ask what they think would make a plane go faster. What would make a plane go slower?

Language Activity

See page 90 for Junior Language Activity sheet; page 91 for Answer Key for Junior Language Activity.

1. Hand out the Junior Language Activity (page 90) sheet and ask the students to write their name on it.
2. Write *propeller* and *prop plane* on the board. Ask students which word comes first in alphabetical order: *propeller* or *prop plane*. Explain that *prop plane* comes first because the first word *prop* ends before the word *propeller* ends, so it is considered to be first in alphabetical order.
3. Ask students to find the word that is first in alphabetical order from the list.
4. Have the students complete the work. Remind students to print neatly and not to rush to finish. You may offer incentives for people who do their work well, without fooling around.
5. Collect the completed Language Activity sheets for the teacher and leave with the answer key (page 91).

Introduce Writing Activity

- Grade 4: Ask students if they have ever tried to break a record, what record they tried to break, and if they were successful or not. Ask: *What kind of records do you think someone could break in an airplane?* (speed, how high you can go, how much weight you can carry, how many times you can fly in a loop in a row, etc.)
- Grade 5: Ask students which is the coolest plane they have ever seen. Ask if they have ever seen planes that have two floors or a bedroom. Have they ever been to an airshow and seen fighter jets? Ask: *What kind of records do you think people try to break in airplanes?* (speed, altitude, distance, etc.)
- Grade 6: Ask students if they would like to be in an airplane doing a roll or a loop. Ask who would like to learn to fly and pilot a plane doing a roll or a loop. What would they need to study to become a pilot? (math, science)

Writing Activity

See page 92 for the Junior Writing Activity sheet.

1. Hand out the Junior Writing Activity sheet (page 92); ask students to write their name on it. Read it over with students.
2. Have students complete the sheet.
   - Grade 4: Remind students to answer the questions in paragraphs and that each paragraph should have at least five sentences.
   - Grade 5: Remind students that they need to write in paragraphs, providing reasons and supporting evidence for their answers. Remind them that paragraphs are a minimum of five sentences, preferably longer. Each question should be answered by at least one paragraph. At minimum, the front of the sheet should be filled before they are finished. Students can use the back of the sheet if they run out of room.
   - Grade 6: Remind students that each question should be answered with a paragraph giving reasons and details supporting their answers. Remind

students to use their own experience and things they have learned from books as supporting details.

3. Collect the Writing Activity sheets for the teacher.

Extra Language Activities

Junior Word Search

See page 93 for the Junior Word Search; page 94 for the Answer Key for Junior Word Search.

Use Extra Language Activity: Junior Word Search sheet (page 93). Ask students to write their name on the sheet.

Junior Crossword

See page 95 for the Extra Language Activity: Junior Crossword.

Use Extra Language Activity: Junior Crossword sheet (page 95). Ask students to write their name on the sheet. Tell students that the answers in the crossword puzzle are the same words as in the Word Search and the Cloze Activity.

- Grades 4 and 5: You can allow students to keep the Language Activity to help them answer the crossword puzzle.

ANSWER KEY FOR JUNIOR CROSSWORD

Across	Down
2. propeller	1. flaps
4. weight	2. prop plane
9. aerodynamics	3. jet
11. elevator	4. wings
13. thrust	5. glider
	6. tail
	7. drag
	8. engine
	10. parachute
	12. lift

Get Ready for Recess

Give students 5 minutes to get ready for recess. Walk students to the door and dismiss them for recess. Make sure there is a teacher on yard duty before allowing them to go outside (or you can go outside with them until a teacher comes out for yard duty).

- Grade 4 students will need only five minutes to get ready in the spring and fall; however, they might need a bit more time to get ready in the winter. Ten minutes should be enough for most classes.
- Grade 6 students will probably need only about 5 minutes to get ready for recess, even in winter. Isn't Grade 6 great? They will take everything they need without being reminded. Of course, there are always the true blue Canadians who would wear a T-shirt in the winter— they are literally blue Canadians! I still insist students take their coats, as they can always take them off outside.

Period 2: Math

Math Game: Beat-the-Teacher Place Value

1. The object of the game is to get the highest number you can.
   - Grade 4: Each student draws a long rectangle divided into five to show the place value for 1s, 10s, 100s, 1000s, and 10,000s.

10,000s	1000s	100s	10s	1s

- Grade 5: Each student draws a long rectangle divided into 6 to show the place value for 1s, 10s, 100s, 1000s, 10,000s, and 100,000s.

100,000s	10,000s	1000s	100s	10s	1s

- Grade 6: Each student draws a long rectangle divided into 7 to show the place value for 1s, 10s, 100s, 1000s, 10,000s, 100,000s, and 1,000,000s.

1,000,000s	100,000s	10,000s	1000s	100s	10s	1s

2. Pull a card out from a deck that has face cards and *10*s removed, or pull a number from 1 to 9 out of a hat. Everyone, including you, decides where they will put this number in their own place-value chart. Everybody keeps their chart hidden.
   - Grade 4: Pull out 4 more cards or numbers one by one (for a total of 5).
   - Grade 5: Pull out 5 more cards or numbers one by one (for a total of 6).
   - Grade 6: Pull out 6 more cards or numbers one by one (for a total of 7).
3. As each card is pulled, everyone decides where each number should go in their own place-value chart. When the numbers have been pulled and placed, ask one student what number they got. Then ask if anyone got a higher number. Continue asking until nobody has a higher number. Then, reveal your number so the students can see if they beat the teacher or not.

Introduce Math Sheet

- Grade 4: Write *8 ÷ 2* on the board. Ask students some ways they could figure it out if they did not know the answer to this question (e.g., drawing 8 dots on the board and circling groups of 2; having 8 counters and dividing them equally into 2 groups). Demonstrate how to do one of the questions in number 4. This might be too difficult for Grade 4 students so encourage them simply to try their best.
- Grade 5: Write a simple double-digit by single-digit multiplication question on the board. Ask one student to come up and solve it. If this is difficult for the class, do a few more examples on the board. Write *24 ÷ 8* on the board. Ask students how they would solve this division question if they did not have the answer memorized (e.g., drawing 24 dots and circling groups of 8; having 24 counters and making 8 equal groups).
- Grade 6: Write an easy double-digit by single-digit multiplication question on the board (e.g., *43 x 3*) and ask if a student would like to come up and demonstrate how to do it. Write a slightly more difficult multiplication question on the board (e.g., *76 x 4*) and ask if someone would like to show how to do it on the board. If there are no volunteers, you can demonstrate it yourself.

Math Sheet

See pages 96–97 for the Junior Math Sheet; page 98 for Answer Key for Junior Math Sheet.

1. Hand out the Junior Math Sheet (pages 96–97); ask students to write their name on it.
2. You might have students start with the graph in #3 first, so that they are up and asking each other questions all at the same time. After 5 or 10 minutes, have students sit down and complete the rest of the sheet.
   - Grade 4: Do the first question of #5 together on the board. Remind students to show their answers in a number sentence and a word sentence.
   - Grade 5: Remind the students to label the columns on the graph and to make a title. Remind them to include their rough work, along with a sentence, to show how they got the answer for the word problems.
   - Grade 6: Let students know they can use manipulatives (e.g., counters) for the division questions. Remind them not to use their phones, that you will be confiscating any phones you see.

Take Up Math Sheet

Grade 4: Start by asking students if they found that they had a pattern in the answers for #2.

1. Have a few students show their 100s chart and the patterns that were made (choose students who have done it correctly). Allow other students to show their graph for #3.
2. Tell students you will be asking each student to answer questions one at a time as you go around the classroom; there is no need to raise hands. If two students in a row don't know the answer, ask if there is anyone in the class who knows the answer to raise their hand.
   - Grade 4: For numbers 1, 4, 5, and 6, go around the room, asking students the answers for the questions. Do the word problems in numbers 7, 8, and 9 together on the board. If many of the students could do the word problems themselves, have one show how he/she got the answer on the board.
   - Grade 6: You may want to do the word problems on the board or have a student demonstrate how to do them.
3. Collect the math sheets for the teacher and leave them with the answer key (page 98).

Get Ready for Lunch

It is a good idea to check with the office to see if Grade 4 students have to be dismissed to an adult.

Students will need about 5 minutes to get ready for lunch. Walk the students to the lunchroom/gym. Dismiss students who go home for lunch from the doors.

Afternoon Routines

Attendance/Joke, Story, Fact, etc.

- Grade 4 Riddles

  Q: What goes up but does not come back down?
  A: Your age.
  Q: What comes down but never goes up?
  A: Rain/snow.

- Grade 5: If there is time and a computer in the class, I run a clip of the movie *Dante's Peak* showing the volcano exploding a cloud of gas and rocks like the one that killed 30,000 people when Mt. Pelée erupted in 1902. If there is no computer, I tell students about Mt. Aso, a volcano in the south of Japan about one hour away from where I used to live. At least once a year, the volcano emits poisonous gases and nobody is allowed to go near it. In September 2015, it erupted with a large ash cloud. Nobody was hurt. It is still active and could erupt at any time. There are people living at the base of the mountain.

- Grade 6: Sometimes I do attendance in Pig Latin or saying the names backwards to see if students can recognize their names. Girls seem to be particularly squeamish around this age, so I love telling gross facts and watching their faces.

Period 3: Science

Setting Up for Science

You will need about 5 minutes to get ready for the Science Experiment. You will need paper, paper clips, and metre sticks. It is best if there is enough material for each person to have their own paper clip and metre stick; however, students may share if they have to. If there are not enough metre sticks to go around, students can use rulers or simply measure using their feet (e.g., the plane flew 5 foot lengths or 10 foot lengths).

Introduce Science Experiment

- Grade 4: Ask students if they remember any of the parts of a plane and what they do from the morning lessons. Ask if they remember any of the things that help a plane fly or hinder a plane from flying. Can they think of ways to help a plane fly faster or longer or higher?
- Grade 5: Ask students if they are good at making paper airplanes: i.e., if they ever made an airplane that flew really, really far; if they ever made planes that do loops or land upside down. Why do they think different paper airplanes fly different ways?
- Grade 6: Tell students that there are World Championships for flying paper airplanes. Ask what they think is the farthest throw for a paper airplane. The longest paper-airplane flight was more than 69 metres; that's about as long as one-and-a-half school buses.

Science Experiment

See page 99 for the Junior Science Experiment sheet.

1. Hand out the Junior Science Experiment sheet (page 99); ask students to write their name on it. Read it over with the class.
2. Discuss rules for flying paper airplanes (e.g., no flying a plane at someone, no being silly or dangerous) and the consequences of breaking the rules: plane is grounded; i.e., taken away.
    - Grade 4: Ask students if they have ideas about how to alter their airplanes; e.g., folding the wings so they are narrower, putting an eraser in it. Discuss how to measure the distance the planes fly from where the student stands to where the plane lands. Explain that the students should not move when they throw their plane until they have started measuring the distance or they will not know where to start measuring.
3. Ask students what kinds of graphs they know: bar graphs, pictographs, line graphs, pie graphs, etc.
    - Grade 4: Demonstrate how to make a graph from information they will have when they have done the experiment.

- Grade 5: Ask how they would make a graph from the information they recorded. If they are having trouble, demonstrate how to make a bar graph from information you make up.
- Grade 6: Ask students what type of graph they think will work well for this experiment and why.

4. Allow students to complete the experiment. Monitor the class for dangerous or silly behavior with the paper airplanes. If necessary, go over the rules and consequences. After 30 minutes of flying paper airplanes, have students work on their graphs.

Take Up Science Experiment

1. Ask students what happened when they put a paper clip on their airplane (it should have gone farther). Ask how they altered their airplane and if it made it go farther or shorter distances. Ask the distance of their farthest flight; ask that student to demonstrate with his/her plane.
2. Ask a few students to show their graphs.
   - Grade 4: Discuss what kinds of graphs are really suited to this information. Collect the papers for the teacher.
   - Grade 6: Have them explain what their graphs show about the data.
3. Collect Science Experiment sheets for the teacher.

Get Ready for Recess

Taking students outside early for recess gives them a bit more time to run around and get rid of excess energy. It will make the art lesson go much more smoothly!

- Grade 4: In cold weather, you may need to remind students that they need to wear their coats (and hats and mitts, if applicable) outside. It doesn't seem to matter what age the students are, some will always want to go outside in a T-shirt!
- Grade 5: If students finish the Science Experiment early, they can take their paper airplanes outside and see how much farther they can throw them outside than inside.
- Grade 6: Walk students to the door to dismiss them for recess unless otherwise noted by the teacher. Usually only intermediate students walk by themselves to their lockers, to recess, etc.

Period 4: Art

Introduce Art Activity

- Grade 4: If students could have their dream airplane, what would it be like? Would it be fast or small? Would it have a games room or a pool? Ask what it would be like on the outside and the inside.
- Grade 5: If students could own their own plane, would they fly in a luxury plane or a jet fighter? If they could have any feature on they wanted on the plane, what would it be: a games room, the ability to go into outer space, the fastest engine in the world?
- Grade 6: Ask students what kind of airplane they would have if they were millionaires. Would it be a large, luxury plane or a small, fast jet?

Art Activity

1. Hand out a blank sheet of paper to each student; ask students to write their name on it.

2. Tell students they will be drawing their dream plane with pencil. They are to draw the inside and the outside of the plane. They are to use shading to show round parts and to show the shadow of the sun. They are to use lines to show movement.
3. If there is time and they have play clay or modeling clay, the students can make a 3D model of their plane.
4. Collect the pictures for the teacher.

Clean Up Classroom/Get Ready to Go Home

If students are mostly finished before the period is over, use the time for a game, as free time, or to tell a scary story as a reward for good behavior or finishing work earlier in the day.

Give at least 10 minutes for students to clean up from art, pick up garbage off the floor, put up chairs, etc. I sometimes give jobs to students; e.g., cleaning the blackboard, cleaning the erasers, etc. When the bell goes, walk the students to the door and dismiss them.

Extra Activities and Games

Grade 4

Seven Up

This classic game is played in primary classes as well.

Choose seven children to come to the front of the room. All the other children sit at their desks with their heads down, eyes closed, and one hand on their desk. The seven children walk around the class; each one touches the head of one of the children at their desks. Once a child is touched, he/she puts up a thumb to show that he/she has already been picked. Once all seven children have picked someone, they go back to the front of the classroom. The teacher tells the children at their desks they can put their heads up now and open their eyes. The children who have been picked stand up. One at a time, they make one guess of who touched their head. If they guess right, they trade places with the person at the front of the classroom. If they guess wrong, the person who touched them gets to stay at the front of the classroom. Once all seven children have guessed, the game starts over again.

Rock, Paper, Scissors Tournament

Everybody gets into pairs and plays one game of Rock, Paper, Scissors. The losers sit at their desks and the winners find another partner to play. The game continues until one person has won. If there is an uneven number of players, make one group a group of three: if all three choose the same thing (e.g., everyone chooses rock) or a different thing (e.g., there is one rock, one paper, and one scissors) they replay; if there are two of a winning choice, the two winners play again to see who goes onto the next round.

Grade 5

Silent Ball

Alternatively, when students make a noise or miss the ball, they get the letter B; the next time they get the letter A; then L; then L. Players have four chances to miss the ball before sitting down. Students given no letters are the winners.

Students all pick spots to stand around the classroom. Throw a ball (eraser, crumpled piece of paper) to one student; that student has to catch it without talking or making any noise. The student then throws the ball to another student. Anyone who talks or makes noise has to sit down. Anyone who doesn't catch the ball or throws badly (you judge whether the throw is bad or not) has to sit down. Then, add more challenges. For example, everyone has to stand on one foot, or throw and catch with only the left hand, or have only one eye open. Continue the game until only one person is left.

Guess the Word

Instead of words from the lesson, this game can be played with animals, famous people, or places—any topic you or the students can think of.

One student comes up to the board and faces the class. Write one word from the lesson on the board behind the student: e.g., *jet*, *glider*, *propeller*, *wings*, etc. The students sitting put up their hands and the student standing picks one student to give a hint. After each hint, the student standing tries to guess what the word is. If the student guesses correctly, he/she trades places with the student who gave the last hint. Repeat with more words.

Grade 6

Two Truths and a Lie

Tell the class three things about yourself: two true things and a lie. For example, *I can ride a unicycle. I have been to the Antarctic. I have a bullet from World War II.* Ask who thinks the first statement is the lie; students raise their hands. Ask the same thing for the second and third statements before revealing which thing was the lie. Students then each take a turn to tell two truths and a lie. Everyone guesses which statement is the lie. (I have not been to the Antarctic, in case you were wondering.)

Four Number 4s

Students have four number 4s. They can use any operation they want on the 4s. The object of the game is for answers to be all the numbers from 0 to 10. For example, $4 - 4 + 4 + 4 = 8$ and $4 + 4 - 4 - 4 = 0$, so now you have the numbers 8 and 0; you need the rest of the numbers up to 10. Students can work alone or in partners or groups, depending on how much noise you want. This is a very challenging game; students probably will not get all the numbers from 0–10, so the person or group with the most numbers wins.

Junior Cloze Activity: Mr/Ms Accident-Prone Teaches about Airplanes

Name: _____ Date: _____

Fill in the blanks using these words:

parachute, aerodynamics, drag, thrust, lift, weight, propeller, engine, wings, flaps, tail, elevator, prop plane, jet, glider

1. Mr/Ms Accident-Prone was showing students the _____ of an airplane at flight school in a flight simulator.
2. Mr/Ms Accident-Prone told students that the engine needs to overcome the _____ or the force air (or birds or people the plane hits) against the airplane.
3. Mr/Ms Accident-Prone turned on the _____ of the plane, but was standing too close and the simulator said he/she would have been sucked in and died!
4. Mr/Ms Accident-Prone tried again and turned on the _____ engine to get _____ to go forward, but forgot to make sure the simulated crew was out of the way and burned them to death.
5. On a smaller _____, Mr/Ms Accident-Prone turned on the _____ to get thrust and chopped up a simulated bird that was sitting there.
6. Mr/Ms Accident-Prone used the _____ on the _____ to change direction but was too close to the ground, so the plane crashed.
7. Mr/Ms Accident-Prone used the _____ on the _____ to go up and down, down, down, to the ground and crashed.
8. Mr/Ms Accident-Prone tried to show students how to get _____ using air currents to go higher when flying in a _____, as there is no engine or propeller.
9. Unfortunately, Mr/Ms Accident-Prone carried too much _____ in his/her stomach to get any lift!
10. Good thing there was a _____ in the simulation when Mr/Ms Accident-Prone jumped out! He/she did forget to pull the cord, though…

Pembroke Publishers ©2016 *Substitute Teaching?* by Amanda Yuill ISBN 978-1-55138-312-5

Answer Key for Junior Cloze Activity: Mr/Ms Accident-Prone Teaches about Airplanes

1. Mr/Ms Accident-Prone was showing students the <u>aerodynamics</u> of an airplane at flight school in a flight simulator.
2. Mr/Ms Accident-Prone told students that the engine needs to overcome the <u>drag</u> or the force of air (or birds or people the plane hits) against the airplane.
3. Mr/Ms Accident-Prone turned on the <u>engine</u> of the plane, but was standing too close and the simulator said he/she would have been sucked in and died!
4. Mr/Ms Accident-Prone tried again and turned on the <u>jet</u> engine to get <u>thrust</u> to go forward, but forgot to make sure the simulated crew was out of the way and burned them to death.
5. On a smaller <u>prop plane</u>, Mr/Ms Accident-Prone turned on the <u>propeller</u> to get thrust and chopped up a simulated bird that was sitting there.
6. Mr/Ms Accident-Prone used the <u>flaps</u> on the <u>wings</u> to change direction but was too close to the ground, so the plane crashed.
7. Mr/Ms Accident-Prone used the <u>elevator</u> on the <u>tail</u> to go up and down, down, down, to the ground and crashed.
8. Mr/Ms Accident-Prone tried to show students how to get <u>lift</u> using air currents to go higher when flying in a <u>glider,</u> as there is no engine or propeller.
9. Unfortunately, Mr/Ms Accident-Prone carried too much <u>weight</u> in his/her stomach to get any lift!
10. Good thing there was a <u>parachute</u> in the simulation when Mr/Ms Accident-Prone jumped out! He/she did forget to pull the cord, though…

Junior Language Activity

Name: _____   Date: _____

Word List

parachute	weight	tail
aerodynamics	propeller	elevator
drag	engine	prop plane
thrust	wings	jet
lift	flaps	glider

1. Put the words in alphabetical order. Use the back of the page if needed.

_____

_____

2. Match the words to the definitions.

a)	parachute	i)	an airplane with a propeller
b)	aerodynamics	ii)	the part that makes the airplane go up and down
c)	drag	iii)	part of the airplane that converts fuel to motion
d)	thrust	iv)	the way objects move through air
e)	lift	v)	an airplane without an engine
f)	weight	vi)	two long, flat parts of an airplane
g)	propeller	vii)	makes the airplane turn
h)	engine	viii)	how heavy something is
i)	wings	ix)	a very fast airplane
j)	flaps	x)	a device that slows a body falling through air
k)	tail	xi)	forward force produced by propellers or gas
l)	elevator	xii)	the back part of the plane that stabilizes it
m)	prop plane	xiii)	upward force
n)	jet	xiv)	a device with rotating blades
o)	glider	xv)	force of air against an airplane

3.   Use each word in a sentence on the back of this paper.

Pembroke Publishers ©2016 *Substitute Teaching?* by Amanda Yuill ISBN 978-1-55138-312-5

Answer Key for Junior Language Activity

1. aerodynamics, drag, elevator, engine, flaps, glider, jet, lift, parachute, prop plane, propeller, tail, thrust, weight, wings

2. a) parachute — x) a device that slows a body falling through air
   b) aerodynamics — iv) the way objects move through air
   c) drag — xv) force of air against an airplane
   d) thrust — xi) forward force produced by propellers or gas
   e) lift — xiii) upward force
   f) weight — viii) how heavy something is
   g) propeller — xiv) a device with rotating blades
   h) engine — iii) part of the airplane that converts fuel to motion
   i) wings — vi) two long, flat parts of an airplane
   j) flaps — ii) the part that makes the airplane go up and down
   k) tail — xii) the back part of the airplane that stabilizes it
   l) elevator — vii) makes the airplane turn
   m) prop plane — i) an airplane with a propeller
   n) jet — ix) a very fast airplane
   o) glider — v) an airplane without an engine

Pembroke Publishers ©2016 *Substitute Teaching?* by Amanda Yuill ISBN 978-1-55138-312-5

Junior Writing Activity

Name: _____   Date: _____

If you were a pilot, what kind of airplane would you fly? Why? Where would you go and why? What kind of tricks would you learn to do, and what kind of records would you try to break?

_____

_____

_____

_____

_____

_____

_____

_____

_____

_____

_____

_____

_____

_____

Pembroke Publishers ©2016 *Substitute Teaching?* by Amanda Yuill ISBN 978-1-55138-312-5

Extra Language Activity: Junior Word Search

Name: _____   Date: _____

A	R	N	C	C	N	O	S	E	T	P	Y	J	M	T
E	D	I	P	R	O	P	P	L	A	N	E	L	N	F
R	H	C	W	K	Q	W	I	O	X	T	V	H	C	I
O	Q	N	B	I	X	A	B	J	Q	U	W	O	Z	L
D	U	G	P	A	N	Z	Y	L	I	A	T	P	A	D
Y	F	B	R	D	L	G	J	F	X	H	E	D	W	H
N	A	W	O	M	R	J	S	I	G	Q	U	P	E	P
A	J	R	P	A	R	A	C	H	U	T	E	D	I	C
M	M	V	E	U	X	T	G	U	Q	F	O	R	G	I
I	Y	X	L	T	D	F	E	W	E	S	G	E	H	G
C	F	F	L	A	P	S	S	C	I	N	J	L	T	E
S	A	G	E	B	T	V	K	M	V	N	G	O	Y	H
E	W	Z	R	K	T	H	R	U	S	T	R	I	Z	A
V	G	L	I	D	E	R	S	T	R	F	P	B	N	M
Z	F	L	K	S	D	L	R	O	T	A	V	E	L	E

Word List

AERODYNAMICS
DRAG
ELEVATOR
ENGINE
FLAPS
GLIDER
JET
LIFT

PARACHUTE
PROPELLER
PROP PLANE
TAIL
THRUST
WEIGHT
WINGS

Pembroke Publishers ©2016 *Substitute Teaching?* by Amanda Yuill ISBN 978-1-55138-312-5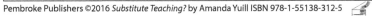

Answer Key for Junior Word Search

A											J		T
E			P	R	O	P	P	L	A	N	E		F
R		W							T				I
O			I										L
D		P		N			L	I	A	T			
Y		R	D		G							W	
N		O		R		S						E	
A		P	A	R	A	C	H	U	T	E		I	
M		E			G							G	
I		L				E						H	
C	F	L	A	P	S			N				T	
S		E							G				
		R		T	H	R	U	S	T		I		
	G	L	I	D	E	R					N		
					R	O	T	A	V	E	L	E	E

Pembroke Publishers ©2016 *Substitute Teaching?* by Amanda Yuill ISBN 978-1-55138-312-5

Extra Language Activity: Junior Crossword

Name: _____   Date: _____

Across

2. a device with rotating blades
4. how heavy something is
9. the way objects move through air
11. makes the airplane turn
13. forward force produced by propellers

Down

1. makes the airplane go up and down
2. an airplane with a propeller
3. a very fast airplane
4. two long, flat parts of an airplane
5. an airplane without an engine

6. the back part of the plane
7. force of air against an airplane
8. part of the airplane that converts gas to motion
10. slows a body falling through air
12. upward force

Pembroke Publishers ©2016 *Substitute Teaching?* by Amanda Yuill ISBN 978-1-55138-312-5

Junior Math Sheet

Name: _____   Date: _____

1. Multiply. Use counters if needed.

1	4	5	8	7	2	3	6	9	4
×3	×2	×3	×1	×2	×6	×3	×1	×1	×4

9	5	3	4	7	5	2	6	8	1
×2	×5	×8	×8	×5	×7	×8	×6	×4	×9

2. Use the first 100s chart to represent counting by 3. Use the second 100s chart to represent counting by 9.

1	2	3	4	5	6	7	8	9	10
11	12	13	14	15	16	17	18	19	20
21	22	23	24	25	26	27	28	29	30
31	32	33	34	35	36	37	38	39	40
41	42	43	44	45	46	47	48	49	50
51	52	53	54	55	56	57	58	59	60
61	62	63	64	65	66	67	68	69	70
71	72	73	74	75	76	77	78	79	80
81	82	83	84	85	86	87	88	89	90
91	92	93	94	95	96	97	98	99	100

1	2	3	4	5	6	7	8	9	10
11	12	13	14	15	16	17	18	19	20
21	22	23	24	25	26	27	28	29	30
31	32	33	34	35	36	37	38	39	40
41	42	43	44	45	46	47	48	49	50
51	52	53	54	55	56	57	58	59	60
61	62	63	64	65	66	67	68	69	70
71	72	73	74	75	76	77	78	79	80
81	82	83	84	85	86	87	88	89	90
91	92	93	94	95	96	97	98	99	100

3. Make a graph of your friends' favorite foods.

Junior Math Sheet (continued)

4. Multiply. Use counters if needed.

10	14	52	80	71	21	33	96	99	42
×3	×2	×3	×1	×2	×6	×3	×1	×1	×4

90	51	31	42	70	51	20	62	82	11
×2	×5	×8	×8	×5	×7	×8	×6	×4	×9

5. Complete the patterns.

511, 521, 531, _____, _____, _____, _____, _____, _____

1040, 1050, 1060, _____, _____, _____, _____, _____

750, 740, 730, _____, _____, _____, _____, _____, _____

90, 94, 98, _____, _____, _____, _____, _____, _____

500, 600, 700, _____, _____, _____, _____, _____, _____

6. Divide. Use counters if needed.

12	4	15	8	16	12	3	6	9	4
÷3	÷2	÷3	÷1	÷2	÷6	÷3	÷2	÷1	÷4

18	25	24	32	35	35	27	6	8	81
÷2	÷5	÷8	÷8	÷5	÷7	÷9	÷6	÷4	÷9

7. Mr/Ms Accident-Prone has 8 packages of thumb tacks. Each package has 25 thumb tacks. How many thumb tacks does Mr/Ms Accident-Prone have in all?

8. Mr/Ms Accident-Prone had 24 thumb tacks. He/she wanted to use the same number of thumb tacks on each of 3 bulletin boards. How many thumb tacks will Mr/Ms Accident-Prone use on each board?

9. Mr/Ms Accident-Prone has 4 packages of 8 bandages. He/she needs to use 2 bandages on each of his/her fingers and toes. Does Mr/Ms Accident-Prone have enough bandages?

Pembroke Publishers ©2016 *Substitute Teaching?* by Amanda Yuill ISBN 978-1-55138-312-5

Answer Key for Junior Math Sheet

1.
1	4	5	8	7	2	3	6	9	4
×3	×2	×3	×1	×2	×6	×3	×1	×1	×4
3	8	15	8	14	12	9	6	9	16

9	5	3	4	7	5	2	6	8	1
×2	×5	×8	×8	×5	×7	×8	×6	×4	×9
18	25	24	32	35	35	16	36	32	9

2.

1	2	**3**	4	5	**6**	7	8	**9**	10
11	**12**	13	14	**15**	16	17	**18**	19	20
21	22	23	**24**	25	26	**27**	28	29	**30**
31	32	**33**	34	35	**36**	37	38	**39**	40
41	**42**	43	44	**45**	46	47	**48**	49	50
51	52	53	**54**	55	56	**57**	58	59	**60**
61	62	**63**	64	65	**66**	67	68	**69**	70
71	**72**	73	74	**75**	76	77	**78**	79	80
81	82	83	**84**	85	86	**87**	88	89	**90**
91	92	**93**	94	95	**96**	97	98	**99**	100

1	2	3	4	5	6	7	8	**9**	10
11	12	13	14	15	16	17	**18**	19	20
21	22	23	24	25	26	**27**	28	29	30
31	32	33	34	35	**36**	37	38	39	40
41	42	43	44	**45**	46	47	48	49	50
51	52	53	**54**	55	56	57	58	59	60
61	62	**63**	64	65	66	67	68	69	70
71	**72**	73	74	75	76	77	78	79	80
81	82	83	84	85	86	87	88	89	**90**
91	92	93	94	95	96	97	98	**99**	100

3. Answers will vary

4.
10	14	52	80	71	21	33	96	99	42
×3	×2	×3	×1	×2	×6	×3	×1	×1	×4
30	28	156	80	142	126	99	96	99	168

90	51	31	42	70	51	20	62	82	11
×2	×5	×8	×8	×5	×7	×8	×6	×4	×9
180	255	248	336	350	357	160	372	328	99

5. 511, 521, 531, <u>541, 551, 561, 571, 581, 591</u>
   1040, 1050, 1060, <u>1070, 1080, 1090, 1100, 1110</u>
   750, 740, 730, <u>720, 710, 700, 690, 680, 670</u>
   90, 94, 98, <u>102, 106, 110, 114, 118, 122</u>
   500, 600, 700, <u>800, 900, 1000, 1100, 1200, 1300</u>

6.
12	4	15	8	16	12	3	6	9	4
÷3	÷2	÷3	÷1	÷2	÷6	÷3	÷2	÷1	÷4
4	2	5	8	8	2	1	3	9	1

18	25	24	32	35	35	27	6	8	81
÷2	÷5	÷8	÷8	÷5	÷7	÷9	÷6	÷4	÷9
9	5	3	4	7	5	3	1	2	9

7. 8 x 25 = 200.
   Mr/Ms Accident-Prone has 200 thumb tacks in all.
8. 24 ÷ 3 = 8
   He/she can use 8 thumb tacks on each board.
9. 8 x 4 = 32, 2 x 20 = 40
   No, Mr/Ms Accident-Prone does not have enough bandages. He/she needs 40 bandages and he/she only has 32.

Pembroke Publishers ©2016 *Substitute Teaching?* by Amanda Yuill ISBN 978-1-55138-312-5

Junior Science Experiment

Name: _____ Date: _____

1. Make a paper airplane. Throw it 3 times. Measure and record how far it goes each time. You can measure in footsteps if there are not enough metre sticks or rulers.
2. Add a paper clip to the front of your plane. Throw it 3 more times; measure and record how far it goes each time.
3. Do one more alteration that you choose yourself. Throw it 3 more times; measure and record how far it goes each time.
4. Put the information into a graph. Make 2 different kinds of graphs.
5. Find out the farthest throws of 5 other students. Make this into a graph.

	1st throw	2nd throw	3rd throw
1st airplane			
Airplane with paper clip			
3rd airplane			

5 students' farthest throw _____, _____, _____, _____, _____

6

Substitute Teaching Intermediate Grades

Grade 7: Kids and Hormones

I was teaching a Grade 7 class for a week; their teacher went on maternity leave early and the principal had been scrambling to find a long-term replacement early. I re-taught some of the math students were supposed to learn the preceding week when they had a different substitute teacher every day. When one of the boys finished his work, he told me this was the first time he'd done his math work all year. I told him that he was quite good at math and I thought it would be worth his time to try because he could probably do quite well. He responded, "Oh, Ms. Yuill, please don't give me hope!"

What Grade 7 Students Are Like

Physically

Adolescents—let's talk about the hyper-hormone years. Do you remember puberty? Really remember? The horrible acne? The mood swings? The inability to get up in the morning? The HUGE importance of every single thing?

No wonder Grade 7 students are so hard to control sometimes; their bodies are out of control. Some of the boys are growing so fast their knees hurt and their arms and legs are out-of-proportion long as they try to get used to this new body. To make it worse, everyone develops at a different pace, so you have teens who look like they're 10 and others who look like they are 18, all in the same class.

Adolescents' feet and hands grow first, then their arms and legs, and then their torsos. This is why some don't seem to fit their feet and others look a bit like monkeys. It also leads to klutziness (no, you can't use this excuse for yourself) and embarrassment. Kids are so sensitive about their bodies at this age, it's best not to bring any attention to them.

Adolescent boys are dealing with surges of testosterone, which brings with it aggression. Grade 7 boys often need to learn strategies to deal with this aggression when it comes out in anger.

Socially

Fitting in with friends is very, very important. It is important not to be too different from the crowd. Students often find a group of friends and those friends have the same interests, use the same slang, and even dress the same. It is in style for boys to wear their pants very, very, very low—much lower than low-rise jeans! I have actually been talking with a Grade 7 boy when his pants fell to the floor. I pretended I was already walking away and not to notice; however, another (male) teacher came over and told him it was not okay to wear your pants so low they fall off. I love the song made famous by an older gentleman on *America's Got Talent*: "Pants on the ground, pants on the ground, looking like a fool with your pants on the ground." Truer words have never been spoken.

Kids are really fun at this age, with a developing sense of humor. You can talk about world events with them. They really appreciate smart wit. Knock-knock jokes kill in Kindergarten and will kill you if you tell them in Grade 7.

Grade 7 students are dealing with the question, *Who am I?* They are old enough to know that they are separate from their parents and can have different thoughts and opinions from them, yet they are still under their parents' authority. They are exploring who they are as independent people.

Academically

The Outsiders, To Kill a Mockingbird, and *Little Women* are books often read in Grade 7. Students are expected to read fluently and with expression when reading aloud. They are able to discuss main ideas and themes in the books and relate them to their own experience.

When writing, Grade 7 students are expected to present their main idea along with supporting arguments and evidence. They are able to revise and improve their first drafts, using symbols and metaphors.

Grade 7 students multiply and divide using fractions and decimals. They use integers and easy algebra. They know how to use exponents and how to find square roots. They are able to solve multiple-step word problems.

How to Teach Grade 7 Well

Although primary and most junior students will like you simply because it is in their nature to like people, Grade 7 students will make you work for it. I find it is important to get intermediate students on your side at the beginning of the day. For this reason, I try not to come down hard on intermediate classes at the beginning in circumstances when I would be quite firm with primary or junior classes. I try to use humor and incentives to get intermediate students to do what they are supposed to do. When I know students a bit better, I use a firmer tone of voice. Of course, if they are hurting someone, I don't hesitate to use a very firm voice!

I find using humor to defuse explosive situations is the best way to go. I tell students,

> You're not supposed to be mean to her/hit him/use bad language/whatever they're doing wrong around a teacher. Don't you know you're supposed to wait until the teacher isn't looking/isn't around before you do that? I was totally standing right here when you did that!

If I have to, I ask the student to leave the class for a few minutes and come back when he/she is calm.

There is a difference between trying to get the students on your side and trying to be their friend. I am their teacher, not their friend. They need me to be their teacher. Even though it is easier to teach Grade 7 when students are on your side,

I used to have the reputation of being the teacher that told not-funny jokes. I liked the kind of stupid jokes and the kids thought it was funny that I thought they were funny when they obviously weren't.

it is still important to make sure that they know there are boundaries and limits. They need to know this and they want to know it—even if it isn't consciously.

As with junior classes, I find that promising they will have free time before lunch or at the end of the day is a good incentive for good behavior. I often start with 20 minutes of free time on the board for intermediate classes and then add or take away minutes, depending on the behavior or noise level. I often take away quite a few minutes right near the beginning before they settle down and then slowly (hopefully) add time back. If it is only one student or group of students making noise, I start awarding extra minutes to individual people. I make sure I have a timer on my phone so that I can give people the exact amount of time I said I would.

Grade 8: King of the Hill

I was teaching Grade 8 English-as-a-Second-Language in Japan. One of the boys was going to inherit his father's rice farm when he was done school. He was not very interested in learning English and told me, "Rice speaks Japanese"; I responded, "Many pretty girls speak English." Another student told me he was learning English so he could speak to me. Ahhhh, yes, thank you!

Students often want to know how old I am. I usually tell them I am 100. The primary students nod their heads and believe I am 100. The intermediate students keep asking my age. If the student is shorter than me (I'm shorter than average), I tell them that I only tell my age to people who are taller than me. They drag over a friend who is taller than me and tell the friend to ask me my age. I then whisper to the friend that I won't tell them my age, but I will tell the other student that I did; they can say they know my age, but I won't tell their friend—it will drive their friend crazy!

What Grade 8 Students Are Like

Physically

By Grade 8, most students are in full-swing puberty, although some boys and maybe some girls start a bit later. Voices are changing, bodies are changing—it's a lot of change. Many students are very self-conscious about the changes and do not want any attention to be drawn to their bodies.

Some kids play-fight; it's part of bonding with your friends, I think (watching it from the outside as an adult just makes me roll my eyes). Sometimes the play-fight can go too far, especially as hormones are raging and bodies are changing. Sometimes kids who play-fight don't know their own strength and can really hurt someone. A sharp word from a teacher will often stop the fight, especially if you catch it at the start and nip it in the bud.

Sometimes girls will need to go to the bathroom quickly. It's important to be aware and sensitive to this. It's also important not to ask too many questions or draw attention to the girl, as she will be easily embarrassed. It's better to err on the side of caution and give Grade 8 girls permission to go to the bathroom.

Some students are already dating by this time. Sometimes there is touching (or kissing) that is inappropriate for school. It is important to let the students know in a sensitive way that certain kinds of touching are not appropriate at school.

Socially

Grade 8s are often the King of the Hill, the top of the mound, the ones on top as the oldest students in the school. They are often given more responsibilities by teachers; e.g., helping run fun days, participating in student government, and having reading buddies in the Kindergarten classes. This is a real source of pride for students, having come so far in their schooling. It can also lead to students thinking it is okay to slack off or to be a bit cocky. It's important to help students find the right balance.

Grade 8 is often the last year before students enter high school. There is a lot of talk about which high school students will go to, what courses they will take, and all things high school. It can be stressful and exciting and sad for students. There are major decisions to make and, most importantly, their friends may not be going to the same school. This is a very big deal for Grade 8 students. Students often become very close near the end of the school year, as it is the last time they will be together with some of their friends and as a class.

Grade 8 students' sense of humor is developing and they can surprise you with really good lines! Sarcasm is a big thing and sometimes a bit overdone. They appreciate unexpected humor or humor with a twist. Of course, they still find toilet humor funny—it never really goes out of style!

Academically

Of Mice and Men, *Animal Farm*, and *Lord of the Flies* are books often read in Grade 8. Grade 8 classes often read books made popular by movies. This can help keep them more engaged in the material. They are able to discuss the main theme of books and give details from the book that support the main idea. They are able to identify the points of view of various characters in the book, as well as their own point of view on the themes of the book.

Grade 8 students are expected to present various points of view in their writing and to provide reasons why they are valid. Students are able to evaluate and discuss various points of view and relate them to their experience, something they have read, or the world at large.

Multiplication and division are done with integers, fractions, decimals, and exponents in Grade 8. Decimals are converted to percentages, as students learn how to solve problems that are found in everyday life. Students solve algebraic equations and plot the answers on a graph.

How to Teach Grade 8 Well

As students bodies are developing, their judgment sometimes lags behind. Some kids make inappropriate comments about girls' bodies, or laugh at a boy who is awkward or whose voice is changing. It is important to keep a respectful atmosphere in the classroom. Often students do not understand the seriousness of their actions and think things are just in fun. Grade 8 kids have a sense of compassion and it is good to tap into it and ask them how they would feel if someone made fun of their bodies like that. It is also important to let them know that inappropriate comments will not be tolerated. Students often have difficulty finding the line between what is funny and what is sexual harassment. If there is a big problem with this in class, I sometimes talk with them about what might be seen as a physical attack; e.g., snapping a bra strap.

As always, and even more with Grade 8 students, humor is a great way to get them involved in a lesson or to get them listening instead of talking out. It's always good to have a couple of jokes or a funny story ready. When students seem to be drifting away from listening and starting their own conversations during the lesson, using a joke is a good way to get their attention back.

Students really want to relate to the teacher, even in Grade 8 when they are cool and don't seem to care about the teacher's opinion. It's good to know a little bit of pop culture so you can talk with the students about it. Using the latest movie, TV show, or pop star trivia in a lesson can set you apart as a great substitute teacher!

Intermediate Day Plan and Lessons

Intermediate Day Plan: Natural Disasters and Human Settlement Patterns Theme

Starting Routines
 Self-Introduction/Attendance/Joke, Story, Fact, etc.: 10 minutes
 Silent Reading: 15 minutes
Period 1: Language
 Introduce Cloze Activity and Language Activity: 5 minutes
 Cloze and Language Activities: 20 minutes
 Introduce Writing Activity: 5 minutes
 Writing Activity: 15 minutes
 * Optional: Students who finish early can do the extra language activities. These can be used at any time students are finished work early during the day.
Get Ready for Recess: 5 minutes
Recess
Period 2: Math
 Math Game: 15 minutes
 Introduce Math Sheet: 5 minutes
 Math Sheet: 40 minutes
 Take Up Math Sheet: 10 minutes
Get Ready for Lunch: 5 minutes
Lunch
Afternoon Routine
 Attendance/Joke, Story, Fact, etc.: 10 minutes
Period 3: Science
 Introduce Science Activity: 10 minutes
 Science Experiment: 40 minutes
 Take Up Science Experiment: 10 minutes
Get Ready for Recess: 5 minutes
Recess
Period 4: Art
 Introduce Art Activity: 10 minutes
 Art Activity: 50 minutes
Clean Up Classroom/Get Ready to Go Home: 15 minutes
Home Time

Starting Routines

Self-Introduction/Attendance/Joke, Story, Fact, etc.

Grade 8 students sometimes saunter in slowly and a bit late with a feeling of entitlement as the oldest kids in the school. I start telling a scary story, and students who are sitting and want to hear the story will shush the late arrivals, saving me from doing it!

- Intermediate students love ghost stories. I often promise to tell a ghost story if they are well-behaved during attendance.
- I make it clear that cell phones are not allowed; if I see or hear any cell phones during the class they will be confiscated until the end of class. Sometimes I make this little speech after I see the first cell phone: I loudly announce how much I need a new phone and how isn't it nice that students have brought their phone for me to class. This usually elicits smiles and the hasty shoving of phones into pockets. Sometimes a student will keep a phone out, saying that I can't take the phone. I respond that they can put it away, give it to me, or take it to the principal, it is their choice.

Silent Reading

Students will have a book they are reading for class or a library book. If not, there are often books in the classroom. If one or two students need to go to their lockers to get their books, I allow that. If it is most of the class, I go with the class to the lockers. If the whole class needs to go get their books because they were not prepared for language first period, I make a judgment call. If the class seems fairly responsible, I go with them to the hallway where the lockers are to get the books and then we return to the classroom. If it is a more difficult class, I skip silent reading and move on to the Cloze Activity; I use the extra language activities if I need to fill in time.

Period 1: Language

Introduce Cloze Activity

- Grade 7: Ask students if they have ever been in a natural disaster, such as an earthquake or hurricane. Ask if they have seen natural disasters on TV or the Internet.
- Grade 8: Ask students if they know the difference between a typhoon and a hurricane. If they don't know, ask if they know what a typhoon or hurricane is. (They are both storms with high winds, but a typhoon starts in the Pacific Ocean and a hurricane starts in the Atlantic Ocean.) Ask if students know any names of hurricanes. Ask if they know how hurricanes are named. (A list of boy and girl names. starting with A to Z, put out by the World Meteorological Organization every year is used.)

Cloze Activity

See page 114 for the Intermediate Cloze Activity sheet; page 115 for Answer Key for Intermediate Cloze Activity.

See Answer Key for Intermediate Language Activity on page 117 for definitions.

1. Hand out Intermediate Cloze Activity sheet (page 114); ask students to write their name on it.
2. Go over the words with students, asking them what they think each word means.
   - Grade 7: If nobody knows what a word means, explain it. Write it on the board with the definition if there is room.
   - Grade 8: With the class, go over what each word in the list means. If there is room, write definitions that students have given correctly on the board.
3. Have students complete the Cloze Activity.
4. Collect Cloze Activity sheets for the teacher and leave with answer key (page 115).

Introduce Language Activity

- Grade 7: Write *population distribution* and *population density* on the board. Ask students which word comes first in alphabetical order. Review what to do when two words start with the same letter or when the first word in a two-word term is the same.
- Grade 8: Ask students which word comes first in alphabetical order (*agricultural area*). Write it on the board. Point out how the two words go together, that each separate word is not put into alphabetical order. Do the same with the second word in alphabetical order. Ask students what to do when there are two phrases with the same first word. (You go by the first letter of the second word, and then the second letter if the first letter is the same, etc.)

Language Activity

See page 116 for Intermediate Language Activity sheet ; page 117 for Answer Key for the Intermediate Language Activity.

1. Hand out Intermediate Language Activity sheet (page 116); ask the students to write their name on it.
2. Point out to the students that in #2 they are to define each word *and* use it in a sentence. Choose a word and do it together on the board.
3. Have students complete the Intermediate Language Activity and collect the completed sheets for the teacher with the answer key (page 117).

Introduce Writing Activity

- Grade 7: Ask students their favorite disaster movie and why. Choose a few students to answer the question.
- Grade 8: If students had to choose a natural disaster to live through, which one would it be and why?

Writing Activity

See page 118 for the Intermediate Writing Activity sheet.

1. Hand out the Intermediate Writing Activity sheet (page 118); ask the students to write their name on it.
2. Have students complete the Intermediate Activity sheets.
   - Grade 7: Ask students to write at least one paragraph to answer each question. If students cannot think of enough to write, tell them they can always answer the question *Why would you do that?*
   - Grade 8: Let them know that, at minimum, they have to answer every question with one paragraph. Remind students that paragraphs are to contain at least five sentences. Encourage students to write not only what they would do but why they would do it. An A+ answer would include evidence to support their answers and go farther than simply answering the questions asked.
3. Collect the Writing Activity sheets for the teacher.

Extra Language Activities

Intermediate Word Search

See page 119 for Intermediate Word Search; page 120 for Answer Key for Intermediate Word Search; page 121 for Intermediate Crossword.

- Use Extra Language Activity: Intermediate Word Search sheet (page 119). Remind students to write their name at the top of the page.
- Tell students that even though some phrases have a space between the words, in the Word Search there will not be a space.

Sometimes I offer incentives for the first person finished or the first row finished, as Grade 8 students may not take word searches or crosswords seriously and simply talk to friends instead of doing their work.

Intermediate Crossword

Use Extra Language Activity: Intermediate Crossword sheet (page 121).

ANSWER KEY FOR INTERMEDIATE CROSSWORD

Across
3. volcano
5. reclaimed land
7. wilderness area
13. spatial technology
15. drought
16. landslides
20. population distribution

Down
1. population density
2. tornado
4. floods
6. avalanche
8. resource town
9. migration
10. linear
11. earthquake
12. agricultural area
14. clustered
17. sustainability
18. scattered
19. tsunami

Get Ready for Recess

Accompany students to their lockers about 5 minutes before the bell will go. If students do not have lockers, let them get their coats and things ready. Stay until the bell goes to make sure nobody stuffs anybody into a locker or starts an Ultimate Fighting Championship in the halls. Dismiss them at the bell, making sure everyone goes outside and nobody stays around the lockers, drawing graffiti of the principal on the walls.

Period 2: Math

Math Game: Count to 100

All students stand up. The class counts to 100, one student at a time. Each student can say one or two numbers; it is their choice. Any student who counts a multiple of 10 sits down and is out. This game is a bit slow at first; however, as students understand the strategy involved and that they can help someone stay standing or get them out, the game becomes more interesting.

Introduce Math Sheet

• Make a T-chart on the board. Ask students who are the oldest children in their families to stand up and record the number with tallies. Do the same for children who are in the middle, the youngest, and only children. Make the T-chart into a bar graph and a pie graph. Discuss other types of graphs and which ones would suit this kind of survey best.

SAMPLE T-CHART

Youngest	Middle	Oldest

108

Sample Bar Graph

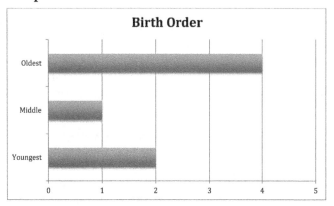

Sample Pie Graph

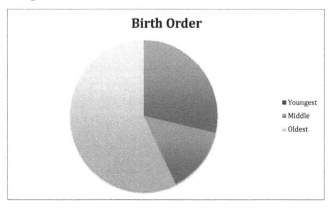

Math Sheet

See pages 122–123 for the Intermediate Math Sheet; page 124 for Answer Key for Intermediate Math Sheet.

1. Hand out the Intermediate Math Sheet (pages 122–123); ask students to write their name on it.
2. Ask for volunteers to demonstrate how to do the second question in #1 on the board. Do the same for number 2a) and number 4a). Ask students if they remember the formula for a perimeter of a circle (2πr). Ask the numerical value of pi/π (3.14) and what r stands for (radius). Ask the formula for the area of a circle (πr2).

Take Up Math Sheet

1. Let students know you will be going around the room, asking for the answers to the questions. There is no need for them to raise their hands to answer.
2. Ask the first student the answer to the first question. If the answer the first student gives is wrong, ask the next student. If the answer is wrong, ask students to raise their hands if they know the answer. Ask the second student the answer to the second question. Continue around the class until all the questions are answered.
   - Grade 7: You may need to do the word problems on the board with the class.
   - Grade 8: Questions that many people found difficult can be demonstrated on the board.
3. Collect the sheets and for the teacher and leave with answer key (page 124).

Get Ready for Lunch

Allow students to get ready for lunch 5 minutes before the bell rings. If students go to their lockers, accompany them until the bell to make sure everyone makes good choices in the hallways; i.e., no running up and down, no chasing each other all over (why do students do that?). Ask students to be quiet in the halls. Once the bell goes, they can go to lunch.

Afternoon Routine

Attendance/Joke, Story, Fact, etc.

Usually by this point in the day I know the names of students who are very helpful and the names of students who require extra attention. At lunch I try to remember the names of students who are generally quieter or who need less attention.

If I get the impression that some students may have switched names when I took attendance in the morning, I just ask one responsible student to help me with afternoon attendance while the class is settling down. I go through the names and that student tells me if those students are present or not. When I get to the names of people I think switched names, I ask the student helping me to point out the students.

Period 3: Science

Introduce Science Experiment

Ask students if they remember the last time the electricity went off at home; allow some students to answer. Ask what they used for light, how they cooked food, etc.
- Grade 7: What is the longest they can remember going without electricity? Ask students if they have ever seen a large demonstration of falling dominoes.
- Grade 8: Ask students if they have ever seen old-fashioned machines that worked without electricity; e.g., a water wheel used to make a mill work at a pioneer village.

Science Experiment

See page 125 for Intermediate Science Experiment.

1. Hand out the Intermediate Science Experiment sheet (page 125); ask the students to write their name on it.
2. Read it together and explain that the eraser will represent the medical supplies they need to move. Brainstorm ways to move objects without electricity (levers, pulleys, gravity). Demonstrate moving an eraser from one desk to a shorter desk by sliding it down a ruler.
3. Go over your Hypothesis (*I can move an eraser along a ruler from one desk to another*), the Objective (*to move an eraser from one desk to another*), the Method (*slide an eraser down a ruler*), Observations (*sometimes the eraser falls off the ruler*), and Conclusions (*this would work if there was a way to keep the eraser from falling off the ruler*).
4. Point out that the method you used only had one part (a ruler) but that they need three parts to their system. Allow students to work by themselves or in groups of up to four.

Take Up Science Experiment

- Grade 7: Ask students to show their system for moving an eraser or other small object, and what their conclusions were. Collect the Science Experiment sheets for the teacher.

- Grade 8: Ask students if anyone would like to demonstrate their system. Ask what difficulties they had and how they overcame them. Collect the Science Experiment sheets for the teacher.

Get Ready for Recess

Students are often getting tired by this time of the day. If there is time, I take students outside for recess early, giving them free time they have earned as an incentive earlier in the day.

Have students clean up from the Science lesson. About 5 minutes before the bell goes, accompany students to their lockers to get ready for recess. Once the bell goes, they may go.

Period 4: Art

Introduce Art Activity

- Grade 7: Ask students if they know of any natural disasters that were well-known. If not, ask them to imagine what would happen if they were in a hurricane or an earthquake. How do they think they would feel?
- Grade 8: Tell students the story of Pompeii, the ancient Roman town destroyed by a volcano and buried in ash. When archaeologists found it, they poured plaster into spaces in the ash where bodies once were, allowing researchers to see what the people looked like and what they were doing at the time of the disaster.

Art Activity

Hand out blank paper; ask the students to write their name on them. Tell students they will draw a natural disaster. They need to show emotion in their work: it will probably include people but doesn't have to if they can find another way to convey emotion. They also need to show movement; for example, a runner about to take another step or a ball dropping. Remind them that they have 50 minutes, so it should be a detailed picture with lots of emotion. Collect the art for the teacher.

Clean Up Classroom/Get Ready to Go Home

I often stop about 20 minutes before the end of the day and allow students to have free time or play a game; or I tell a ghost story if they have done well.

When there is 10–15 minutes before the end of class, ask students to clean up their desks and the floor, making sure it is neat for their teacher's return. I often have students pick up five pieces of garbage each.

Extra Activities and Games

Grade 7

Boys vs. Girls

I often play a boys vs. girls game for points. I ask girls questions that typically boys would know the answers to; I ask boys questions that typically girls would know the answers to. I give two points for a correct answer. If a team doesn't get the answer, I allow the other team to answer for one point.

Questions for Girls:
- Name one Canadian Football League team besides the one in your home city. (BC Lions, Calgary Stampeders, Edmonton Eskimos, Saskatchewan

Roughriders, Winnipeg Blue Bombers, Hamilton Tiger-Cats, Montreal Alouettes, Ottawa Redblacks, Toronto Argonauts)

- What is a caulking gun? (tool used to fill in cracks in windows and bathtubs with a white putty-like substance)
- What is a Phillips head screwdriver? (one with an x or a + head)
- How many points is a touchdown? (6 points)
- What is a Spyder (spelled with a Y)? (a classic sports car)

Questions for Boys:
- What is a French manicure? (natural/pink nails with white tips)
- What is the purpose of a slip? (to prevent skirts from being see-through and/or to prevent static cling)
- What is the difference between a pig tail and pony tail? (a pig tail is a braided pony tail)
- What is a loofah? (a spongy, hand-held skin scrubber)
- What is the purpose of foundation? (to even skin tone and/or cover blemishes)

True or False

This game is played in rows or teams. I ask true or false questions based on the lesson just given or on general knowledge. Every person in the class is asked one question (to make the teams even, sometimes a student answers twice). Before the question is asked, the student can choose 1 point, 2 points, or 3 points. If they get the answer right, they get 1, 2, or 3 points for their team/row. If they get the answer wrong, 1, 2, or 3 points are taken away from their team's score. Some examples of questions:

- A volcano is a vent in the earth's crust. (T)
- A flood is a big wave. (F)
- Population distribution is the arrangement of people living in an area. (T)
- An agricultural area is a farming community. (T)
- Reclaimed land is property given back to its original owners. (F)

Grade 8

Guess Who

One student comes to the front of the class and imitates a famous person or a teacher in the school. Stress to students that they are not to insult the person/teacher, nor to be rude, but simply to imitate what that person says and does. The other students guess who it is.

Would You Rather...?

One student comes to the front of the class. I ask a question that starts with, "Would you rather..."; e.g. *Would you rather be able to walk on water or breathe under water?* The student puts his/her hands behind his/her back and puts up 1 finger for the first option (walk on water) or 2 fingers for the second option (breathe under water). Everyone in the class does the same thing, based on what they think the person at the front will say. Say, "Go," and everyone holds up their fingers to see who in the class guessed correctly. Students can keep track of how many points they have for correct guesses. Some examples of questions:

Would you rather…
- have purple hair or silver hair?
- live on a boat or in a recreational vehicle?
- be the smartest person or the best-looking person in the room?
- have 10 siblings or no siblings?
- lose all your hair or all your teeth?
- be super-strong or super-fast?
- have everything smell very strong or taste very strong?
- be able to instantly speak another language or speak to animals?
- ride in a spaceship or a submarine?

Intermediate Cloze Activity: Population Distribution and Natural Disasters

Name: _____   Date: _____

Fill in the blanks using these words:

sustainability, reclaimed land, migration, population distribution, population density, linear, scattered, clustered, resource town, agricultural area, wilderness area, spatial technology, volcano, landslides, tsunami, earthquakes, floods, tornados, avalanche, droughts

1. Mr. and Mrs. Too-many-children have a very high _____ _____ in their small house.
2. Sometimes the population of children is _____ at the top of the stairs and there is an _____ of children down the stairs.
3. Sometimes Mrs. Too-many-children wishes she could use _____ _____ like GPS to find all her children when their population is _____ around the house.
4. Mr. Too-many-children wonders about the _____ of his family, as the _____ _____ he works in is running out of money trees.
5. He is considering taking a job as Pluto at Tokyo Disneyland, but he is worried because the _____ _____ acts like jello in the many _____ there.
6. But the Pluto job is preferable to the cowboy job he considered in a _____ _____ that has _____ and _____—not to mention that he's allergic to (scared of) horses, cows, and wind.
7. Mrs. Too-many-children would like to take a job in an _____ _____ in a cabbage farming town where the _____ _____ is _____, following the Gold Coin River.
8. But when the Gold Coin River _____, it does cause _____ in Gold Bar Town.
9. Recently there has been a _____ of people from Gold Bar Town to Million Dollar View Beach, even after the _____ caused it to be called Big Wave Beach.
10. In the end, Mr. and Mrs. Too-many-children decide to stay in Money Tree City with its dormant _____; it seems like the safest place to live.

Pembroke Publishers ©2016 *Substitute Teaching?* by Amanda Yuill ISBN 978-1-55138-312-5

Answer Key for Intermediate Cloze Activity: Population Distribution and Natural Disasters

1. Mr. and Mrs. Too-many-children have a very high <u>population density</u> in their small house.
2. Sometimes the population of children is <u>clustered</u> at the top of the stairs and there is an <u>avalanche</u> of children down the stairs.
3. Sometimes Mrs. Too-many-children wishes she could use <u>spatial technology</u> like GPS to find all her children when their population is <u>scattered</u> around the house.
4. Mr. Too-many-children wonders about the <u>sustainability</u> of his family, as the <u>resource town</u> he works in is running out of money trees.
5. He is considering taking a job as Pluto at Tokyo Disneyland, but he is worried because the <u>reclaimed land</u> acts like jello in the many <u>earthquakes</u> there.
6. But the Pluto job is preferable to the cowboy job he considered in a <u>wilderness area</u> that has <u>droughts</u> and <u>tornados</u>—not to mention that he's allergic to (scared of) horses, cows, and wind.
7. Mrs. Too-many-children would like to take a job in an <u>agricultural area</u> in a cabbage farming town where the <u>population distribution</u> is <u>linear</u>, following the Gold Coin River.
8. But when the Gold Coin River floods, it does cause <u>landslides</u> in Gold Bar Town.
9. Recently there has been a <u>migration</u> of people from Gold Bar Town to Million Dollar View Beach, even after the <u>tsunami</u> caused it to be called Big Wave Beach.
10. In the end, Mr. and Mrs. Too-many-children decide to stay in Money Tree City with its dormant <u>volcano;</u> it seems like the safest place to live.

Pembroke Publishers ©2016 *Substitute Teaching?* by Amanda Yuill ISBN 978-1-55138-312-5

Intermediate Language Activity

Name: _____   Date: _____

Word List

sustainability	clustered	tsunami
reclaimed land	resource town	earthquake
migration	agricultural area	flood
population distribution	wilderness area	tornado
population density	spatial technology	avalanche
linear	volcano	drought
scattered	landslide	

1. Put the words in alphabetical order. Use the back of the page if needed.

   _____

   _____

2. Define each word and use it in a sentence. Use the back of this page if needed.

   _____

   _____

   _____

   _____

   _____

   _____

   _____

   _____

   _____

   _____

   _____

   _____

   _____

Answer Key for Intermediate Language Activity

1. agricultural area, avalanche, clustered, drought, earthquake, flood, landslide, linear, migration, population density, population distribution, reclaimed land, resource town, scattered, spatial technology, sustainability, tornado, tsunami, volcano, wilderness area

2. • sustainability: living within the limits of available resources
   • reclaimed land: new land made from bodies of water using methods such as landfill or dams
   • migration: the permanent shift of people from one place to another or the seasonal movement of people or animals from one place to another
   • population distribution: the pattern of where the people live within a given area
   • population density: the number of people in a particular area
   • linear: in a straight line
   • scattered: in no pattern
   • clustered: closely spaced in groups
   • resource town: a community that forms around and whose economy is based on a natural resource; e.g., fish, coal, pulp
   • agricultural area: a place where crops are grown
   • wilderness area: a place in its natural state with minimal impact from people
   • spatial technology: digital tools that support the use of geographic data; e.g., geographic information systems (GIS), the global positioning system (GPS), and remote sensing
   • volcano: a mountain that erupts with lava, ash, and rock
   • landslide: large amounts of the ground move down a hill, slope, or mountain
   • tsunami: a very large wave
   • earthquake: the shaking of the surface of the earth
   • flood: when a body of water overflows, causing dry land to be underwater
   • tornado: high, destructive winds that form a funnel
   • avalanche: snow and ice falling down a mountain

Some definitions taken from Ontario Curriculum documents.

Pembroke Publishers ©2016 *Substitute Teaching?* by Amanda Yuill ISBN 978-1-55138-312-5

Intermediate Writing Activity

Name: _____   Date: _____

How would you survive a natural disaster? Where would you go? What would you do? How would you feel? Who would you help?

_____

_____

_____

_____

_____

_____

_____

_____

_____

_____

_____

_____

_____

_____

_____

_____

_____

_____

_____

_____

Extra Language Activity: Intermediate Word Search

Name: _____   Date: _____

A	S	F	T	F	V	P	O	P	U	L	A	T	I	O	N	D	E	N	S	I	T	Y	W	S
F	T	W	I	L	D	E	R	N	E	S	S	A	R	E	A	D	Z	T	V	S	O	J	D	P
B	F	R	D	O	P	O	B	G	X	A	S	Q	U	I	E	T	G	M	F	I	H	C	P	A
K	I	E	S	O	J	E	R	K	S	G	S	O	F	C	N	E	L	G	A	O	W	P	X	T
U	N	W	A	D	Y	G	H	S	T	H	G	U	O	R	D	R	Q	U	N	V	O	D	E	I
J	V	X	L	S	S	I	C	Z	D	S	K	B	S	J	O	Q	U	H	K	T	B	O	Y	A
Z	M	A	Q	U	S	C	I	B	L	T	P	F	Y	T	S	E	D	I	L	S	D	N	A	L
E	A	R	T	H	Q	U	A	K	E	S	L	H	P	M	A	R	Q	U	F	U	P	A	O	T
Y	E	F	O	R	N	J	H	T	W	V	Y	C	T	N	W	I	M	C	E	N	D	C	P	E
G	R	E	P	P	A	G	X	Y	T	Z	Q	U	X	I	C	L	N	D	Y	A	V	L	C	C
P	A	W	T	O	L	K	B	J	G	E	R	X	J	K	Z	V	X	A	K	M	T	O	I	H
E	L	Z	H	C	W	B	F	H	E	Y	R	N	G	B	S	B	R	K	B	I	A	V	J	N
N	A	D	V	Q	U	E	D	D	N	P	L	E	W	I	V	C	S	X	L	I	Q	N	B	O
Q	R	T	T	O	R	N	A	D	O	S	F	C	D	O	T	Z	T	I	H	G	L	U	M	L
W	U	Q	Z	W	S	V	L	J	I	N	E	A	D	H	T	J	N	A	Z	L	M	I	R	O
A	T	P	U	A	Y	F	K	C	T	I	D	M	Z	O	W	E	I	E	M	I	G	W	T	G
M	L	R	J	G	L	V	I	T	A	E	F	P	B	G	A	F	C	A	Y	R	X	N	X	Y
O	U	O	H	N	B	X	M	K	R	M	E	O	W	R	Q	U	H	R	A	G	M	M	H	C
X	C	Z	Q	U	T	Y	H	E	G	L	Q	U	N	J	Y	S	Z	T	U	L	N	F	D	M
R	I	Y	V	A	S	E	T	C	I	K	D	K	Y	Q	U	Z	I	V	T	O	T	D	K	X
D	R	X	G	M	T	S	F	G	M	F	M	C	H	E	R	O	W	L	Z	C	S	A	E	L
H	G	P	W	L	U	O	D	J	N	O	R	L	P	K	N	V	Z	Q	U	O	P	E	W	G
I	A	V	A	L	A	N	C	H	E	N	D	N	A	L	D	E	M	I	A	L	C	E	R	Y
N	I	B	C	K	C	J	N	S	R	A	J	X	B	K	I	S	T	S	B	I	R	A	J	V
N	O	I	T	U	B	I	R	T	S	I	D	N	O	I	T	A	L	U	P	O	P	L	B	H

Word List

AGRICULTURAL AREA	LINEAR	SUSTAINABILITY
AVALANCHE	MIGRATION	TORNADOS
CLUSTERED	POPULATION DENSITY	TSUNAMI
DROUGHTS	RECLAIMED LAND	VOLCANO
EARTHQUAKES	RESOURCE TOWN	WILDERNESS AREA
FLOODS	SCATTERED	POPULATION DISTRIBUTION
LAND SLIDES	SPATIAL TECHNOLOGY	

Pembroke Publishers ©2016 *Substitute Teaching?* by Amanda Yuill ISBN 978-1-55138-312-5

Answer Key for Intermediate Word Search

1	2	3	4	5	6	7	8	9	10	11	12	13	14	15	16	17	18	19	20	21	22
			F	P	O	P	U	L	A	T	I	O	N	D	E	N	S	I	T	Y	S
		W	I	L	D	E	R	N	E	S	S	A	R	E	A						P
		O																			A
		O							S												T
		D			S	T	H	G	U	O	R	D							T		I
		S	S		C					T	S	E	D	I	L	S	D	N	A	L	A
E	A	R	T	H	Q	U	A	K	E	S						A			U		L
E						T								I			N			C	T
R						T										N			A	L	E
A								E								A			M	O	C
L							R	N										B	I	V	H
A						N		E	W									L	I		N
R		T	O	R	N	A	D	O	S		D	O			I			L		M	O
U							I			T						N			I		L
T							T		D						E		G		T		O
L							A	E				A			C			R			G
U							R					R				R	A				Y
C							E	G									T	U			
I					T		I						I				O				
R			S				M					O					S				
G			U									N							E		
A	V	A	L	A	N	C	H	E	D	N	A	L	D	E	M	I	A	L	C	E	R
		C																			
N	O	I	T	U	B	I	R	T	S	I	D	N	O	I	T	A	L	U	P	O	P

Pembroke Publishers ©2016 *Substitute Teaching?* by Amanda Yuill ISBN 978-1-55138-312-5

Extra Language Activity: Intermediate Crossword

Name: _____ Date: _____

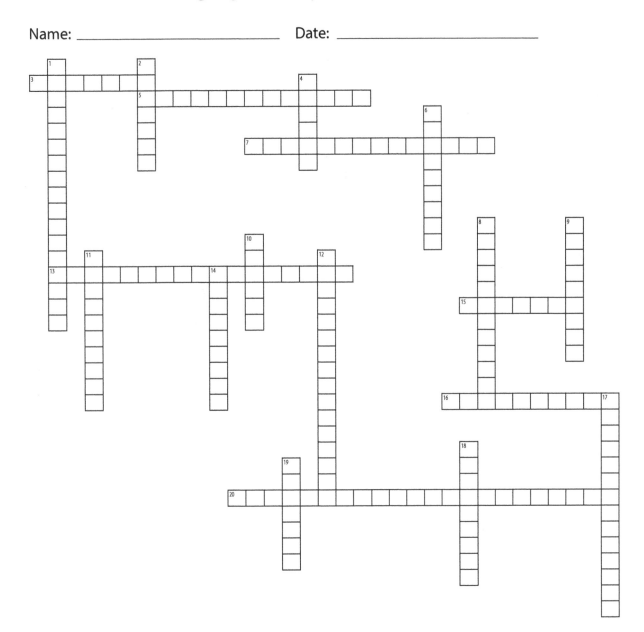

Across

3. a vent in the earth's crust
5. land that was in poor condition that has been improved so that it can be used
7. an uninhabited region
13. software or hardware that interacts with real world locations
15. a long period of dry weather
16. the falling of a mass of soil
20. the arrangement of people living in a given area

Down

1. the number of people living per unit of area (e.g. square kilometre)
2. whirlwind
4. overflow of water
6. large mass of falling snow
8. a community around an industry
9. the permanent movement of people from one area to another
10. arranged in a line
11. a tremor or shock
12. a farming community
14. close together
17. not depleting natural resources
18. dispersed
19. a big wave

Pembroke Publishers ©2016 *Substitute Teaching?* by Amanda Yuill ISBN 978-1-55138-312-5

Intermediate Math Activity

Name: _____   Date: _____

1. Multiply.

10	14	52	80	71	21	33	96	99	42
×63	×82	×34	×12	×25	×67	×31	×17	×10	×47

90	51	31	42	70	51	20	62	82	11
×25	×54	×83	×82	×59	×78	×87	×66	×54	×94

2. Calculate.

a) $678 \times 10 =$ _____   b) $678 \div 10 =$ _____   c) $678 \times 0.1 =$ _____

c) $496 \div 0.1 =$ _____   d) $496 \times 0.01 =$ _____   e) $496 \times 1000 =$ _____

f) $13 \div 100 =$ _____   g) $13 \times 0.001 =$ _____   h) $13 \div 0.001 =$ _____

i) $1024 \times 100 =$ _____   j) $1024 \div 100 =$ _____   k) $1024 \div 0.1 =$ _____

l) $3 \div 1000 =$ _____   m) $3 \times 1000 =$ _____   n) $3 \times 0.001 =$ _____

3.
Use a T-chart and tallies to make two kinds of graphs showing in which months your friends celebrate their birthdays. Use the back of this page if necessary.

4. Use long division to divide.

a) $5\overline{)100}$ b) $6\overline{)1024}$ c) $9\overline{)693}$ d) $3\overline{)852}$ e) $7\overline{)749}$

f) $2\overline{)774}$ g) $4\overline{)1024}$ h) $8\overline{)986}$ i) $5\overline{)875}$ j) $3\overline{)357}$

k) $9\overline{)555}$ l) $7\overline{)391}$ m) $6\overline{)275}$ n) $8\overline{)190}$ o) $6\overline{)350}$

Pembroke Publishers ©2016 *Substitute Teaching?* by Amanda Yuill ISBN 978-1-55138-312-5

Intermediate Math Activity (continued)

5. Find the perimeter and the area of each shape. Use the back of this sheet if needed.

a)

25 m

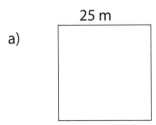

b)

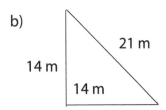

14 m

21 m

14 m

c)

25 m

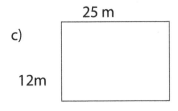

12m

d) radius = 8 m

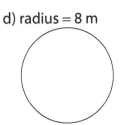

6. Two-thirds of Mrs. Too-many-children's grandchildren have the flu. She has 21 children and each of them have 6 children. How many people are sick?

7. Mr. Too-many-children needs to buy diapers. One brand of diapers has 20 diapers for $8.99. Another brand offers 50 diapers for $20.84. Which one is the better deal?

Pembroke Publishers ©2016 *Substitute Teaching?* by Amanda Yuill ISBN 978-1-55138-312-5

Answer Key for Intermediate Math Sheet

1.

10	14	52	80	71	21	33	96	99	42
×63	×82	×34	×12	×25	×67	×31	×17	×10	×47
630	1148	1768	960	1775	1407	1023	1632	990	1974

90	51	31	42	70	51	20	62	82	11
×25	×54	×83	×82	×59	×78	×87	×66	×54	×94
2250	2754	2573	3444	4130	3978	1740	4092	4428	1034

2. a) $678 \times 10 = 6780$ b) $678 \div 10 = 67.8$ c) $678 \times 0.1 = 67.8$
   c) $496 \div 0.1 = 4960$ d) $496 \times 0.01 = 4.96$ e) $496 \times 1000 = 496{,}000$
   f) $13 \div 100 = 0.13$ g) $13 \times 0.001 = 0.013$ h) $13 \div 0.001 = 13{,}000$
   i) $1024 \times 100 = 102{,}400$ j) $1024 \div 100 = 10.24$ k) $1024 \div 0.1 = 10{,}240$
   l) $3 \div 1000 = 0.003$ m) $3 \times 1000 = 3000$ n) $3 \times 0.001 = 0.003$

3. Answers will vary.

4.
   a) $5\overline{)100}$ = 20   b) $6\overline{)1024}$ = 170R4   c) $9\overline{)693}$ = 77   d) $3\overline{)852}$ = 284   e) $7\overline{)749}$ = 107

   f) $2\overline{)774}$ = 387   g) $4\overline{)1024}$ = 256   h) $8\overline{)986}$ = 123R2   i) $5\overline{)875}$ = 175   j) $3\overline{)357}$ = 119

   k) $9\overline{)555}$ = 61R6   l) $7\overline{)391}$ = 55R6   m) $6\overline{)275}$ = 45R5   n) $8\overline{)190}$ = 23R6   o) $6\overline{)350}$ = 58R2

5. a) $P = 25m + 25m + 25m + 25m$
        $P = 100\text{ m}$
        $A = 25m \times 25m$
        $A = 625m^2$
   b) $P = 14m + 14m + 21m$
        $P = 49m$
        $A = 14 \times 14 \div 2$
        $A = 98\text{ m}^2$
   c) $P = 25m + 25m + 12m + 12\text{ m}$
        $P = 74\text{ m}$
        $A = 25m \times 12m$
        $A = 300\text{ m}^2$
   d) $P = 2 \times 3.14 \times 8m$
        $P = 50.24m$
        $A = 3.14 \times 8^2$
        $A = 200.96\text{ m}^2$

6. $21 \times 6 = 126$, $126 \times \tfrac{2}{3} = 84$
   84 people are sick.

7. $\$8.99 \div 20 = \$0.4495$, $\$20.84 \div 50 = \$0.4168$
   50 diapers for $20.84 is a better deal.

Pembroke Publishers ©2016 *Substitute Teaching?* by Amanda Yuill ISBN 978-1-55138-312-5

Intermediate Science Experiment

Name: _____   Date: _____

The electricity has gone off because of a natural disaster. You need to move large quantities of medical supplies. Working by yourself or in partners or groups, make a system to move an eraser (or something small) from one desk to another. For example, you can move an eraser from one desk to a shorter desk by connecting the two desks with a ruler and sliding the eraser down the ruler. Your system needs to have at least 3 parts. Then, change one part of the system and observe how it affects the whole system. (The system does not need to still work when you change one part.) Describe the function of each component of the system. Use the back of this page if you need more room to write.

Hypothesis

_____

Materials

_____

Objective

_____

Method

_____

_____

_____

Observations

_____

_____

_____

Conclusions

_____

_____

7

Substitute Teaching Beyond the Three Rs

French: Parlez-Vous Francais? Non?

I picked up a music job in a school I didn't know. I like music and I'm comfortable teaching it. When I got to the school, it was a French Immersion school—they forgot to mention that in the message. I was supposed to teach music in French. I didn't think I could keep up with the students in French with my decades-old, rusty, Grade 12 French. Well, I faked it through the day and the students seemed to have fun and they sang—in French!

Tips for Teaching French

There are often CDs that go with the workbooks. The CDs do practically all the teaching you need. If you can find the CDs, I highly recommend using them. If not, there are often dialogues in the French book. Students can read these in partners. You can have them come up and act out a dialogue or read it aloud in turns. You can also have the students memorize them. If there are no workbooks at all, you can play the math flash card game in French: all you need are the flash cards and to know numbers in French (see the list in margin on page 128). If you cannot find the CDs or workbooks, you can use this lesson plan.

Lesson Plan

Materials Needed:
White paper
Pencils

French Lesson Plan

Self-introduction/Attendance/Joke, Story, Fact, etc.: 10 minutes
Bingo: 20 minutes
Introduce Dialogue Activity: 5 minutes
Practice Dialogue: 15 minutes
Present Dialogue: 10 minutes
French Word Search: 10 minutes
Clean up and get ready for recess/lunch: 5 minutes

It is very rare that you would have a 70-minute French lesson, so you probably won't need the whole plan. It is also very, very easy—even if you don't know a word of French, you can use it. This lesson can be used for all grades. The older grades will find it very easy but it is also very fun so they shouldn't get bored.

Self-introduction/Attendance/Joke, Story, Fact, etc.

If you have a story about France or something French, this is the time to tell it. Even better, if you have a story about trying to learn French or having a difficult time learning French, the students will love it. I tell the story of driving through Quebec as a child and at every roadside stop, the menu started with the words *Casse Croute.* My mother wondered what kind of food it was and so she asked what it meant. It turns out it means, "Snack Bar."

Bingo

Many French classes have Bingo cards and the students can tell you where they are. If not, hand out sheets of paper and have the students make a 5 × 5 table, with *B-I-N-G-O* across the top. They use only half the paper to do this. They pick numbers between 1 and 10 and put them under each letter. They tear the rest of the paper into small pieces to mark squares when they are called.

While they are doing this, you will need to write *B1, B2, B3,* etc., up to *B10*, on small pieces of paper. Do the same with *I, N, G,* and *O.* Put all the small pieces of paper into a hat or bag. Pull out one piece of paper and call out the letter and number. Note that *B* is pronounced "bay," *I* is pronounced like a long *e, G* is pronounced "jay" with a soft *g* sound, and *O* is the same as in English.

If you don't want to call out the letters and numbers, choose a student to call them out. Assure the student there will be more than one game and they will have a chance to play as well. Often a student will volunteer for this job.

When you have called out a letter and number, the students who have that letter-number combination on their card cover it with a piece of paper. When one student has a line covered—horizontal or vertical—that student has won. Or you can play so that the whole card has to be covered before anyone can win.

It makes the game more interesting if you offer small prizes—stickers or candy. You can play this game many times and you may find that you only have time for Bingo.

Introduce Dialogue Activity

Tell students they will practice the dialogue you write on the board. Tell them it is an easy dialogue and they may find they can memorize it. They are to practice saying the dialogue in a normal voice, a sad voice, an angry voice, a happy voice, a scared voice, etc. They are to pick the voice they like the best to present to the class.

Practice Dialogue

Have students get into pairs, or you can pair them yourself. If needed, there can be one group of three. Write this dialogue on the board and allow students time to practice it, reminding them that they need to practice using many different voices.

> A: Bonjour.
> B: Bonjour.
> A: Comment t'appelle-tu?

Sample BINGO Card

B	I	N	G	O
2	6	7	2	3
9	5	8	1	6
4	2	4	6	10
1	10	5	3	9
5	1	6	8	2

In French the numbers are:
1: un
2: deux
3: trois
4: quatre
5: cinq
6: six
7: sept
8: huit
9: neuf
10: dix

B: Je m'appelle (insert your name). Comment t'appelle-tu?

A: Je m'appellle (insert your name). Ca va?

B: Oui, ca va, et tu?

A: Ca va.

(Younger children can end the dialogue here.)

B: Veux-tu manger de la crème glacee?

A: Mais oui, allons-y!

Translation:

A: Hello.

B: Hello.

A: What's your name?

B: I'm _____. What's your name?

A: I'm _____. How are you?

B: I'm fine, and you?

A: I'm fine.

B: Would you like to eat ice cream?

A: Yes, let's go!

Present Dialogue

Ask students to come up one group at a time and present their dialogue, using one of the voices they practiced. Have the other students guess which voice they are using. This usually makes for a very funny class, so you may have to remind the class to settle down at the end of each dialogue.

French Word Search

See page 143 for French Word Search; page 144 for Answer Key for French Word Search.

If there is still time left in the class, you can use the sheet on page 143. It can make it more fun if you offer incentives to the students who are done first; e.g. they don't have to help clean up the floor, or they get free time while others are working and cleaning.

Clean Up and Get Ready for Recess/Lunch

There will be little papers all over the floor if you played Bingo. It is a good idea to have students pick them up and put them in recycling so the French teacher or caretaker isn't annoyed with you when they see the room. It is a good idea to find out the dismissal procedure from another teacher or from the office; sometimes the homeroom teacher will come and collect the students and sometimes the French teacher takes them to their next lesson. If you don't know, the responsible students will tell you.

Physical Education: Don't Hit Him in the Head with the Ball!

I was teaching a Grade 2 gym class and we were outside to practice Track and Field for the upcoming area-wide competition. We were sitting on wooden benches outside the school as I was taking attendance when, all of a sudden, many of the students were up and running around. They weren't running to the track or sand pits but just haphazardly dashing around the schoolyard. I was about to call them back when I saw them—lots of wasps who made their home under the benches that we had disturbed! We all ran away. It was the best warm-up ever!

Tips for Teaching Phys Ed

Go with comfortable shoes and a whistle. With younger students, make sure they walk into the gym and sit down in their regular spot (usually in a circle, in lines, or in front of a bench). If you don't tell them to do this before they go into the gym, they will run into the gym and run in a circle until they fall down from exhaustion. Try it and see—I'm not kidding! Older students often get changed and will take as long as possible. This is when I hand out incentives for students out of the change room first and to the first team (older students often sit in teams) ready. If you don't make older students sit down, they will go into the equipment room (which they aren't allowed to do, no matter what they tell you), take out basketballs, and shoot baskets. Again, I'm not kidding—just stand there and say nothing and watch. It's like something in their DNA tells all students what to do when there is a substitute teacher. How else would they all know to do the same thing? A secret society?

If students can tell you what they are working on in phys ed and you are comfortable teaching it, it's most helpful to the teacher if you continue with whatever students have been working on. If you are not comfortable, then follow this lesson plan.

Lesson Plan

Phys Ed Lesson Plan

Self-Introduction/Attendance/Joke, Story, Fact, etc.: 10 minutes
Change-up Tag: 10 minutes
Soccer Tournament: 25 minutes
Sideline Soccer: 25 minutes
Get a drink and get ready for recess/lunch: 5 minutes

Materials Needed:
Soccer ball or utility ball (at least 1; 3 is better)

Gym classes are often around 40 minutes; sometimes intermediate gym classes are longer. All ages like these activities and the only equipment needed is a ball (or two or three balls). Even if there is no equipment available, it is usually possible to scrounge up a ball. These activities can be played outside if the gym is not available (and the gym teacher is home with a headache due to paint fumes).

Self-Introduction/Attendance/Joke, Story, Fact, etc.

Students really like gym and don't want to sit around talking for a long time at the beginning—even to listen to a ghost story! I often keep this part of the lesson short so that we can get to all the running around (and yelling).

Change-up Tag

Students find a spot in the gym not too near anyone. Call out an attribute; e.g., brown hair, wearing blue, etc. Everyone with that attribute chases everyone who does not. When students are tagged, they sit down on the spot; they can use their arms to tag others but they cannot move from their spot. After a minute or so, blow the whistle and have everyone stop and stand up. Call out another attribute and the game repeats.

The fun part of this game is when the students are waiting to hear which attribute will be called next, to see if they will chase or be chased. Some attributes to use:

- short hair
- wearing lace-up shoes
- wearing words on your clothes
- freckles
- name starts with letter *A*
- oldest child in the family
- brushed your teeth today
- have a pet

Soccer Tournament

Divide the class into teams of about five or six. Usually elementary classes will have about four teams and junior or intermediate classes will have about six teams. Use pylons or whatever you can find to mark the goals.

Teams play three-minute soccer games (or five-minute games if you prefer) in a round-robin tournament. For example, teams A and B play each other, then teams C and D. If you have four teams, the tournament schedule would be like this:

A vs. B
C vs. D
A vs. C
B vs. D
A vs. D
B vs. C

You can then repeat the whole thing or have semi-finals and finals. With six teams, the tournament schedule would be this:

A vs. B
C vs. D
E vs. F
A vs. F
C vs. B
E vs. D
A vs. D
C vs. F
E vs. B

You probably wouldn't have time for more games than that.

Sometimes, before I pick teams, I allow students to choose which league they would like to be in: competitive or recreational. Students pick which league they would like to be in and then I make teams within those leagues. This allows serious soccer players to play all-out, and those who are not so serious to enjoy playing without the intensity.

Some notes about this tournament:

- Make sure the teams have a specific place to sit when they are not playing, as sometimes good players tend to drift onto teams with other good players and you end up with uneven teams.
- Remind students that the soccer ball stays on the floor in this tournament.
- You are the referee, so if someone purposely trips or kicks someone else, give the ball to the opposite team's goalie.
- It's not necessary to know all the soccer rules, just the important one that there are no hands allowed in soccer. You may have to remind the primary students of this quite a bit at the beginning.

Sideline Soccer

For more on this game, go to Physedgames.com

If the students get tired of the soccer tournament, you can play sideline soccer. Divide the class into two teams. Each team stands along opposite walls of the gym (like they are standing on the sidelines). The whole wall is the goal and everyone on the team is goalkeeper. Five students from each team play soccer, aiming at the goal while the rest of the team members play goalkeeper. After a couple of minutes, the five players become goalies and five more people from each team play. Continue until everybody has had a chance to play. You can play this game with one soccer ball or two or three balls. As with regular soccer, when there is a goal, the goalie throws the ball back into the game. Again, it is important to remind the students that the ball stays on the floor for this game. If there are too many students and it is difficult to get a goal, you can tell the goalies they cannot use their hands to stop goals.

Get a Drink and Get Ready for Lunch/Recess

Students will probably be asking to get a drink part way through the lesson. Sometimes I stop halfway through for a five-minute drink break as we all go to the drinking fountain. At the end of the lesson, students will definitely need a drink, so remember to allow some time for that. You may also need to walk students to their next class, to the lunchroom, or out for recess, or you might have to dismiss them. The students will tell you the regular routine. If they need to return to their classroom or lockers to get coats, leave 10 minutes to do that.

Music: Please Don't Make Me Sing!

I think music teachers are the most likely to leave a video for the students to watch when they are away. They never know if they will get a substitute who knows how to teach music and so it's just easier to leave a video. I have spent many days reading my book as class after class watches the same video the music teacher left. How many times can you watch *Peter and the Wolf* in one day? At least five or six times, it seems! Be sure to bring something to read!!

Tips for Teaching Music

If it's vocal music, there is often a CD. You can simply play the CD and have students sing along. Or they may have songbooks; all you have to do is start the song or ask someone to start the song and everyone will join in (except for the clowns in the back row who fool around, at worst, or just mouth the words, at best). If the teacher left nothing and you don't like singing, you can always play Hangman with musical words: e.g., *song*, *notes*, the name of a song, *quarter note*, *rest*, etc.

If it's instrumental music, by all means skip the instruments unless you have taught instrumental music before. If not, you're just asking for trouble—what was the teacher thinking, not leaving seat work? The students will switch instruments for sure, try ones they want to try, then put them away wrong. Or they will all play at once and you won't be able to get their attention. Or they will fool around and break the instruments. I was a music teacher and, unless I knew the substitute coming in and that they could teach music, I always left seat work or a video— one that was educational and had to do with music, of course!

If you cannot find out what the teacher has been doing or you do not feel prepared to teach that, use this lesson plan.

Lesson Plan

<table>
<tr><td>

Music Lesson Plan

Self-Introduction/Attendance/Joke, Story, Fact, etc.: 10 minutes
Groups of 2, 3, 4 Game: 15 minutes
Moving with Music: 20 minutes
Pictures of Music: 20 minutes
Clean up and get ready for recess/lunch: 5 minutes

</td></tr>
</table>

Materials Needed:
CD player and CD, or radio, or MP3 player, or some other way of playing music

Music, art, and dance are the subjects most likely to have a double period; i.e., two periods at a time are scheduled for these subjects so that the teacher can get more done. Music is more likely to be a 70-minute period than other classes. Students usually like music and so they are more likely to be cooperative, especially when they find out they have such a fun substitute. It is easier for students to get out of control or be too loud in a music class, so you want to make sure your rules are clear at the beginning and to make them aware of cues you use to get them to listen; e.g., let them know that when you clap a rhythm, they are to clap back the same rhythm.

Self-Introduction/Attendance/Joke, Story, Fact, etc.

I like using interesting music facts when I teach music. For example, students often don't know that Mozart wrote "Twinkle, Twinkle Little Star" when he was five or six years old. I also ask if the students know Beethoven's Symphony No. 5. If I can, I play a YouTube video of it for them. I ask if they knew that Beethoven became deaf and wrote a lot of music that he never actually heard.

Groups of 2, 3, 4 Game

I play music as students walk around the music room. It is a sad music room that does not have a CD player or a radio or a computer—something you can play music on. At random times, I stop the music and say a number. Students have to get into groups of that number. If I call out "Four", students have to get into groups of four. With younger children, I don't call out numbers bigger than four. With older students, any number is okay, although numbers lower than ten are the most fun. If you like, students in the last group are out until the next round. However, I often play so that everyone keeps on playing. I start the music again and everyone walks around again until I stop the music and call out another number.

Moving with Music

Tell students they will use the front of their paper for this activity and the back of the paper for the next activity. Play a school-appropriate piece of music, and have students draw a continuous line around the page that represents how the music is moving. For example, students may draw a straight line that curves and then turns into zigzags and then swirls. The line cannot stop and the pencils must stay on the page. Encourage students to draw the line slowly, as most songs are three to five minutes long. Once the song is done, have students stand up with their paper and spread out across the room. Play the song again and have students move around the room in the way their line moves around their page. It is important to tell students to always keep an eye out for other students as they look at their paper and move—it can cause a few collisions! When this is done, ask students to trade their paper with a partner. Play the song again and have students move around the room in the way the line on their partner's paper goes. When we are finished, I ask students if following their partner's line was harder than following their own. They almost always say yes. I ask why they think that is.

Pictures of Music

Students turn over their piece of paper. If there are markers, pencil crayons, etc., in the class, put them out around the room. Play some music—it can be the music used for the last activity or another piece of music. Ask students to draw a picture of how the music makes them feel, the story they feel is being told in the music, or something the music reminds them of. They will have about 15 minutes; play the music over and over. They are to draw a detailed picture. When the time is over, ask students to share their pictures one at a time and explain why they drew what they did. Ask students to put their name on their picture and collect them for or the teacher.

Get Ready for Lunch/Recess

The students will let you know the regular routine; i.e., if their teacher comes to pick them up from music or if you are to take them to class or dismiss them to recess, to lunch, or for the end of the day. It is a good idea to find this out at the beginning of class in case you need to take the students back to their room to get their coats and backpacks before you dismiss them.

Dance: Jump, Jump Around!

I was covering a leave for a dance/music teacher. She and the principal had arranged for two professional hip-hop dancers to work with the students for two weeks to teach each class their own hip-hop dance routine. So I was paid to learn hip-hop dance from two professionals from 8:45 a.m. to 3:15 p.m. for two weeks. Then I was to continue working with each class to perfect the routines before a hip-hop dance concert! Did I mention that I am a white, middle-aged woman? Yo, yo! This is how we do it!

Tips for Teaching Dance

Even primary children seem to smell worse after dance/movement. Trying to get intermediate boys to dance (except for the occasional break-dancing superstar) is like pulling teeth. Fortunately, there are usually CDs in the dance room and often DVDs that you can just put on. Students already know the dance and they will follow the music or the video. If there is nothing, you can allow students to choose groups, make up a dance routine, and then present it—even without music. If there is nothing else, you can use this lesson plan.

Lesson Plan

Materials Needed:
Found objects around the classroom; e.g., pencils, rulers, books

---

Dance Lesson Plan

Self-Introduction/Attendance/Joke, Story, Fact, etc.: 10 minutes
Introduce Stomp Routine: 10 minutes
Practice Stomp Routine: 35 minutes
Present Stomp Routine: 15 minutes
Clean up and get ready for recess/lunch: 5 minutes

This tends to be a loud lesson that students really, really enjoy. Definitely tell students that when you turn the lights off and on to get everyone's attention, they are to stop what they are doing, be quiet, and listen to you. With younger students, I tell them that they are to put everything down and put their hands on their heads, as it is oh-so-tempting to make more noise!

Self-Introduction/Attendance/Joke, Story, Fact, etc.

In 1518 in France, the Dancing Plague killed many people. People danced until they collapsed and died of heart attack, stroke, or exhaustion. Authorities thought that the only way to cure the people of this dance mania was to have them dance more, so they built a stage and hired musicians to play music!

Introduce Stomp Routine

Tell the students that Stomp is a group from England that performs music and dance with found objects. They use garbage cans, basketballs, and kitchen utensils in their routines. If there is access to a computer and the Internet, show a short YouTube clip of Stomp. Usually many of the students have seen Stomp videos or have heard of the group.

Clap a short, simple rhythm. Have students practice clapping the rhythm with you. Tell them they are to join in clapping with you when you tell them to. Start clapping the rhythm by yourself. Have one student join in. Then have a few students join in. Last, have the whole class join in. Do this without breaking the rhythm. It may take a couple of tries, but the end effect is pretty cool.

Tell students that they will be making up Stomp routines with found objects in the classroom. Explain that they cannot use musical instruments or accessories like drumsticks; only things not normally used in making music. Tell students that, in groups, they will have about 30 minutes (or 20 minutes if it is a shorter class) to make a routine that they will present to the class. They need to make sure that they include movement in the routine and not simply stand in one place the whole time.

Practice Stomp Routine

Give groups of four to six students places to practice in the room. Make sure that students are using appropriate found objects, not the clock from the teacher's

135

desk or something like that. Younger students may need a bit of help getting started, so you give them a rhythm they can use. If the music room is fairly bare, there might not be a lot of found items in the room. In this case, students can use their own bodies to make music: their hands, feet, shoes, etc. Including movement in the routine can be challenging. As students work on their routines, you can walk around and give suggestions about how they can move; e.g., they could add a turn or a spin between rhythms, or slide side to side while clapping. When there is about 10 minutes left, let students know that they need to start finalizing their routines. Emphasize that it is more important to do a short routine well than to do a longer routine that not everyone in the group knows.

Present Stomp Routine

Have students come up, one group at a time, and present their routines. In my experience, some of the routines are barely there, but others are very, very impressive! Of course, junior girls often make up dances during recess and lunch, so they have a bit of an advantage.

Clean Up and Get Ready for Recess/Lunch

Students often need a drink at the end of this class. After they have cleaned up the classroom and put all found items back in their place, I usually take them to the water fountain. Find out from students if their teacher comes to pick them up or if you drop them off somewhere. Other teachers can also help you with the regular routine.

Drama: Haven't I Had Enough Drama Today?

I was teaching drama for the day in a middle school. I had Grade 7 and 8 students and the teacher had left plans for them to work on a small play in groups. There were a lot of students and not a lot of space in the classroom. It was especially loud when everyone was practicing. So I allowed a couple of groups to work in the hallway. When I went into the hallway to check on how they were doing, none of the students were around. They had all skipped class. So, I don't recommend allowing students to work in the hallway, even if it is loud and crowded in the classroom…

Tips for Teaching Drama

Students think of drama as a free period, usually. And if you don't want to teach drama, it might be tempting to think of it that way yourself. Drama often involves a lot of games, which is good. If students are working on a play or presentation, you can give them a work period. If they are not working on anything, you can play an easy game. There is always the Name/Animal game. You sit in a circle and think of an animal that starts with the same letter as your name. The first person says their name and the animal, and does an action and noise to go with the animal. The second person says their name and the animal, and does the action and noise; then says the first person's name and animal, and repeats the action and noise. The third person does their own name, animal, and action/noise, then the second person's, and then the first person's. This continues until the last person does everyone's name, animal, action, and noise. Or you can follow this lesson plan.

Lesson Plan

Materials Needed:
Winsome personality ;)

Drama Lesson Plan

Self-Introduction/Attendance/Joke, Story, Fact, etc.: 10 minutes
Darling-Won't-You-Please-Smile Game: 10 minutes
Story with Tableau: 25 minutes
Famous Story/Movie Tableau: 25 minutes
Get ready for recess/lunch: 5 minutes

As with most subjects, primary and junior drama will often be an approximately 40-minute lesson. Sometimes intermediate students will have a longer drama lesson. Students usually like drama because it involves a lot of games. Sometimes they are shy and it may take some convincing to get them to participate. This is when I use incentives! Everyone who participates gets an incentive.

Self-Introduction/Attendance/Joke, Story, Fact, etc.

Drama lends itself to telling stories, so I often tell a couple of good stories: one scary and one funny, or one touching and one true. Students of all ages love a good story. I especially try to use different voices for different characters, actions, and voice variations to enhance the stories. This sets the tone and it allows students to be braver in drama when you have already demonstrated it!

Darling-Won't-You-Please-Smile Game

Students sit in a circle with one student in the middle. The student in the middle goes up to another student and says, "Darling, won't you please smile?" That student has to reply, "Darling, I just can't smile," without smiling. The student asking is allowed to do anything except touch the other person; they can make noises, make faces, etc. If the student replying doesn't smile, the student in the middle goes to someone else. If the student does smile, that student is now in the middle.

Story with Tableau

A tableau is a frozen picture. Students use their bodies to make a still picture from a story, movie, book, etc.
- Tell younger children the story of The Three Little Pigs; periodically, stop and ask the children to make a tableau of one of the characters in the story. The children stand up and individually use their bodies to create a frozen picture of one character. At the end of the story, divide children into groups of three or four. They have to come up with a tableau for one scene in the story. When all the groups have come up with a tableau, each group presents their tableau one at a time. The other children guess which scene they are showing.
- With older children, tell a well-known story from a book or movie; e.g., *Charlotte's Web*, *Romeo and Juliet*, or *The Wizard of Oz*. Or tell a story that they may not know or a story from history; e.g., the Underground Railroad. Divide students into groups of four or five. As you tell the story, stop partway through and ask the groups to make a tableau of that scene. Give them a couple of minutes to work it out. Each group presents their tableau.

Famous Movie/Story Tableau

For this activity, students should be in groups of four to six. Tell students they can pick which story/book/movie they want to represent in a tableau. They are to pick a scene which the rest of the class will recognize. Give students 5–10 minutes to get ready. Then, each group presents their tableau. The other students guess which story/book/movie the scene is from. If there is time, allow them to do it again.

Get Ready for Lunch/Recess

The students will let you know the regular routine; i.e., if their teacher comes to pick them up from Drama or if you are to take them to class or dismiss them to recess, to lunch, or for the end of the day. It is a good idea to find this out at the beginning of class in case you need to take the students back to their room to get their coats and backpacks before you dismiss them.

Art: No, You Can't Use the Scissors to Cut Your Hair!

We had been using scissors to cut paper in a Grade 1/2 class. It turns out that's not the only thing we were cutting that day. I started finding patches of hair around the room—blonde, black, and brown. I started looking at the students to see who matched the samples I had collected. I even held up the patches to some students to compare the color. Then I saw him. The black hair. He had definitely cut his hair. I found the others as well and wrote notes in their agendas to their parents explaining what had happened. I probably didn't need to explain to the parents of the child with black hair. Anyone could just look and see what had happened!

Tips for Teaching Art

Often teachers have art projects that last two or three classes, especially with intermediate students. If the students are partway through an art project, they can simply continue. If they are finished, I ask them to add more detail or to help a friend who is still working. There are often craft materials in the art room. You can replicate something you've done before with the materials: draw a picture/ paint a picture/cut and paste. Whatever's in the room, use it. I love art, the kids love art—it's great! If you're not sure what to do, you can use this lesson plan.

Lesson Plan

Materials Needed:
White paper
Pencils
Construction paper in different colors
Glue
(No scissors!)

Art Lesson Plan

Self-Introduction/Attendance/Joke, Story, Fact, etc.: 10 minutes
Ripped-Paper Picture: 50 minutes
Clean up and get ready for recess/lunch: 15 minutes

Even in primary grades, art lessons are usually longer than 40 minutes, and often up to 75 minutes. Most children really like art and this makes it easier to teach. It can take a few minutes for children to settle down and get going. Once they are involved, I sometimes put on music to listen to while they do their art. I also let the students sit where they want and chat with their friends, as long as it doesn't get too silly or loud.

Self-Introduction/Attendance/Joke, Story, Fact, etc.

I sometimes tell the story of how the Mona Lisa was stolen in 1911 from the Louvre in Paris, France. A man walked into the Louvre and saw that the room was empty. He lifted the Mona Lisa off the wall and took it to a nearby stairwell. He removed the frame, wrapped his smock around the painting, and walked out the door! He kept it for two years before being caught. He claimed he wanted to return the painting to Italy, as the artist, Leonardo da Vinci, was Italian. The art thief went to jail—but only for seven months, and many Italians considered him a hero!

Ripped-Paper Picture

Students draw a very simple picture on a piece of paper in light pencil. They rip very small pieces of construction paper and glue it onto the picture. The end result is a picture that looks like a collage or a mosaic (see sample in margin). These pieces often look quite good, even if the students aren't that skilled. It is best if students work with one color at a time, and finish using the construction paper of that color before going onto the next color. It is also best if they rip a piece of paper and then glue it, then rip the next piece of paper and glue it. If they rip everything first, they may rip too much paper and waste it. If they glue everything first, the glue goes dry and is also wasted.

Clean Up and Get Ready for Recess/Lunch

This can be a really messy activity, as ripped pieces of paper seem to find their way to the floor, the shelves, the teacher's desk, and the students' hair. It is really amazing how skilled students are at spreading paper around a room! So I leave about 10 minutes to clean up the room. Also, students tend to get glue on their hands in this activity, so I allow them to wash their hands after the ripped paper is picked up and the classroom is clean. If there is no sink in the room, I send them to the bathroom in groups of three or four.

As always, the students will let you know their regular routine. If you are to dismiss the students to recess or at the end of the day, be sure to dismiss primary students when a teacher is on yard duty or to their parents/guardians. If you are dismissing them to lunch, be sure to walk them to the lunchroom. Intermediate students are usually allowed to go to their lockers by themselves, but it is good to check with another teacher to be sure.

Other Subjects/Classes: I'm Teaching What?!

Help! I'm teaching instrumental music in French or something else I know nothing about—okay, grammar police, about which I know nothing. Sometimes you pick up a job and when you get to the school you find out it's a French Immersion school or that the drama job is really prep coverage including physical education and computer lab. Or sometimes it's even worse—Grade 8 math (Didn't I take this stuff in university? Aren't the answers in the back of the book anymore?).

One day I arrived at a school to teach Kindergarten for the day and found out that it was a behavioral kindergarten class. I didn't even know that existed! That day, one student was sent home for soiling his pants—apparently he did this often and used it as a control technique. Another student used a swear word I haven't even heard a Grade 8 student use—in context! That day was quite an education—for me.

The truth is that there are so many subjects you may be required to teach, I don't even know them all! You may be asked to teach English as a Second Language, Special Education, Computers, Library, Religious Education, Sex Education, Gifted classes, Geography, History, Juggling, Tight-Rope Walking, or many, many others! It is impossible to be prepared for them all, but it is possible to have a few tricks up your sleeve to make things a bit easier.

Of course, if there is time, the principal or secretary will tell you which teacher will know what the absent teacher is currently doing in class. That teacher can often give you ideas about what to do. And of course, once you have a recess or a lunch, there is time to find out what the teacher has been doing, or at least to photocopy some of the reproducible pages from this book. The problem comes when it is the beginning of the day and there is no time and no plan. Your secret weapon in this case is silent reading! After your self-introduction, attendance, and joke, or story, or gross fact, have students read silently. Ask one or two students the regular routines and what they are doing in that class. If the students don't know, they will tell you which student to ask. Everyone in every class knows which student the teacher chooses to help all the time! There are often textbooks you can follow or projects the class is working on. If at all possible, keep to the routine and lessons that students already know and are working on. If it is not possible, once you do have a plan, have students put away the books they are reading and continue on with the plan. Here are some ideas to help you with some of the subjects you are likely to be asked to teach.

Special Education

There are two types of Special Education classes. One is where the students are withdrawn from their class and come to you for one or two periods to get help. The other is where you have the students for the whole day.

Students who are withdrawn from their class often come with math or language that they are working on in their class; you can simply help them with the materials they bring. If they do not bring anything, you can ask what they are working on and help them with that if you are comfortable doing so. If not, you can use the drama lesson plan from page 136; the students have fun and they will be practicing their language skills.

Special Education classes where you have the students all day can be classes of behavioral students, developmentally delayed students, and children with learning disabilities. These classes normally also have an Educational Assistant or an Early Childhood Educator who knows the routine and what the students are working on, and is able to help you plan something for the day. The problem comes when both the teacher and the EA/ECE are away on the same day. In that case, I usually start the day with games (and songs, if it is a primary class) and then have silent reading so I can look around the teacher's desk and ask students to help. If there is nothing of help, you can use the primary (page 50) or junior day plan (page 77) along with the reproducible pages.

History

History is usually taught only in intermediate classes and often has a textbook or a workbook. You can often just ask students what page they are on and simply do the next page. These pages also often include questions or activities. If there are no questions, you can put questions on the board about the pages the students read that day and have them answer the questions. You can also ask students to act out the history that they read that day.

Geography

Geography is usually taught only in intermediate classes. There is usually a textbook or a workbook that students are working through. When you find out where they are, have students read the next lesson and work on it. If there are no questions with the lesson, make up questions and write them on the board while the students are doing their reading for the day. You can also play the Geography game. Say the name of a place. Then a student has to say a place where the name starts with the letter that your place ended with. For example, if you say, "Toronto," then the student has to say a name of a place that starts with an O. Continue around the room until all the students have had a chance to say a place.

Social Studies

In primary and junior classes, History and Geography are called Social Studies. They usually have textbooks or workbooks and you can simply do the next page. The added advantage of social studies is that often the workbook pages can be colored; if it is not clear what the students are working on, you can have them color the pictures in their workbook or color the work that they have already finished.

English as a Second Language

Students are usually withdrawn from their classroom for ESL. Sometimes they come with work they are doing in their own classroom and you can help them with that. Sometimes the ESL teacher has a program for them and they can show you what they are working on. If there is nothing for them to do, it is often fun to play games. Really anything you do in English will help them, so you can play Tic-Tac-Toe or Hangman and they will learn and have fun.

Computers

Students love computers! It is far and away their favorite class! It is also a fairly easy class to teach. If the teacher has left no plans and students say there is nothing specific they are working on, I have students go to www.coolmath-games. com, a fun site where students learn math while playing. All grades seem to enjoy it. I do not let the students go to YouTube, Facebook, or their email. They must go to a site that is approved or I do not let them use the computer.

Library

Often the most difficult thing about the library is figuring out the system for signing books in and out. Sometimes it is very easy. Sometimes students know how to do it. Sometimes students simply aren't able to exchange books until the teacher comes back. Library is fairly easy because students find a book to read and read it. If it is a younger class, I often pick a book off the shelves and read it to them before allowing them to find a book to read themselves. Sometimes the most difficult part of library is having students read quietly and not chat or fool around.

Language, Math, Science

Of course, if the teacher leaves seat work, everything's okay. It's when they actually want me to teach something I don't know that there's a problem. In that case, if I can fake it, I will. In the event that I really can't fake it, I ask the students to be the teacher. For example, I ask students to do the first question on the board and explain how they did it. We continue with the next question, and the next, until most of the students (and I) understand. I also allow students to work in groups to figure out the answers.

These subjects are all covered in chapters 3 to 6, and you can use the lesson plans and reproducible pages there if the students are not able to tell you what they are working on.

Students of all ages like it when the teacher reads a book to them. If the class is already reading a book, you can read the next chapter. If not, you can start reading a book and leave it for the teacher with a note if you are not able to finish. After reading a book, you can have students write what they think happened to the characters next. Or they can draw what they think happened to the characters next.

No matter what you do, as long as nobody dies, the principal will be happy that you filled in when there was no lesson plan and that you had the initiative to do something—anything, especially if it was educational! You can give yourself a pat on the back!

In good weather, you can take the students outside for Daily Physical Activity (DPA) time or you can play active games in the classroom.

French Word Search

A	C	W	R	M	A	Z	Y	W	R	W	X	P	N	T
B	O	N	J	O	U	R	N	A	J	K	O	G	A	M
V	M	Y	U	B	U	R	F	U	Q	Y	J	P	F	T
X	M	T	C	Q	L	Q	K	V	Z	L	P	I	E	A
D	E	J	C	Z	E	E	W	G	L	E	X	N	I	D
K	N	B	M	A	D	C	E	K	L	Z	O	H	G	X
G	T	T	I	O	V	X	M	L	G	A	B	I	W	S
C	L	F	S	G	N	A	E	F	U	V	C	M	Z	A
K	T	J	P	S	P	I	R	Y	L	O	D	E	I	H
E	M	A	I	S	H	Y	C	E	A	C	Z	H	E	Y
S	H	U	H	M	G	A	L	L	O	N	S	Y	U	B
A	D	Q	E	I	G	O	S	F	J	P	L	Q	X	V
F	O	R	N	F	U	D	Q	U	X	B	P	R	U	C
R	L	B	C	E	C	O	D	U	N	T	B	W	E	S
P	E	L	L	E	P	P	A	M	V	K	T	M	V	J

ALLONS Y   MAIS
BONJOUR   MAPPELLE
CAVA   OUI
COMMENT   TAPPELLE
CREME   VEUX
GLACEE

Pembroke Publishers ©2016 *Substitute Teaching?* by Amanda Yuill ISBN 978-1-55138-312-5

Answer Key for French Word Search

	C													T
B	O	N	J	O	U	R							A	
	M											P		
	M										P			
	E		C				G		E					
	N			A		E		L						
	T				V	M	L		A					
					A	E					C			
						R						E		
	M	A	I	S		C							E	
						A	L	L	O	N	S	Y		
				I									X	
				U									U	
				O									E	
	E	L	L	E	P	P	A	M					V	

Pembroke Publishers ©2016 *Substitute Teaching?* by Amanda Yuill ISBN 978-1-55138-312-5

8

On the Way to the Job You Want

When No Schools are Calling

This is all great advice, you may be thinking, *but how can I use it when I only get called once or twice a month to come in and be a substitute?* Yes, at the beginning, it's often difficult. So here are a few tips for those frustrated and *slightly* panicky would-very-much-like-to-be-working-most-days-before-I-cannot-pay-the-rent teachers.

First of all, print out your résumé with a cover letter. Take them to schools near you, ask for the vice-principal, or the principal if there is no vice-principal (the vice-principal is usually the one who deals with substitute teachers), and give him or her your résumé. Be sure to mention in person and in the cover letter that you are on the substitute list, live close by, and are willing to come in last-minute. This is like music to a vice-principal's ears. If the principal or vice-principal is not there, leave your résumé with the secretary and ask when the principal or vice-principal will be there. Return when they are at school and ask if they got your résumé. A five-minute conversation can make the difference between working four times a month and working four times a week.

Schools are much more likely to ask you to come in when they know you. So networking can be a great way in. Talk with teachers you know and ask them to request you. Ask your friends to introduce you to teachers, vice-principals, principals, or secretaries they know. People are usually eager to help out. Schools are always looking for good substitutes. Schools sometimes have enough substitutes, but rarely have enough really good substitutes—which is what you are! (Or at least what you're going to be if they would only call you.) Don't feel bad about handing out your name and number. When teachers know you are looking for work, they will often ask you if you are available on a day they already know they will not be at work.

Getting to know a school by volunteering is also another great way in. You can co-lead a co-curricular activity with a teacher (this way, if you are a bit late because you are coming from another school, it will not matter as much). Any day you are not working, volunteer in a classroom at one of the schools close to you. You will often get half-day jobs on the spot when a teacher feels sick and will go home only because she/he knows you can take the class.

Schools have lunchroom supervisors: people who come in over the lunch hour to supervise children while teachers are on lunch. These people also get sick sometimes. If you can get onto the substitute list for lunchroom supervisors and go to a job, you can let the school secretary know that you are also on the substitute teacher list.

Not only lunchroom supervisors, but also Educational Assistants get sick and need a day off sometimes (it's like an epidemic or something!). If you are able to get on these substitute lists, you may get more work and get to know people in the schools. The more teachers and school administrators you know, the more likely you are to get called for a substitute teaching job.

I know people who became Educational Assistants as their permanent job when they were unable to get a job as a substitute teacher. They got to know the school and worked there for a year. The next year, they were able to get substitute teaching jobs with the support of the principal of the school where they were an Educational Assistant. It's all about getting a foot in the door and getting known.

Lastly, certain times of the year are slow for everyone: September, January, after spring break—basically the beginning of the term. The last week of the school year is also slow. December is often very busy.

Plan for it to be a bit slow when you first start. Be patient. Or bribe the vice-principal (okay, this doesn't really work). As you get experience and find your own style and get better and better, you will get more jobs. Again, be patient. I know some substitute teachers who had jobs to supplement their income at the beginning, jobs that were not during school hours. If being a teacher is what you want to do, you will make it work. You will make it (just in case you're starting to doubt).

One Day Turns into Two...

Many jobs turn out to be more than one day. Principals often ask if you are available the next day to take the same class. "Sure, I can cover this class again tomorrow and the next day, and all year, if you need…" I try not to sound too desperate when I quickly agree to take the next day as well. Of course, I may regret it three weeks later when I've agreed to take 38 Grade 7 kids at a school over an hour's drive from my place. Sometimes you're looking for a foot in the door that just does not want to open easily!

Don't feel bad saying no if you already have a job for the next day or if you were heading out to the cottage. No explanation is needed; a simple "I'm so sorry, I'm not free tomorrow" will suffice. However, this does fall under the category of try-to-do-it-if-you-can. It can only lead to a better relationship with the principal and the school, and therefore more opportunities. Many sick leaves have been covered by teachers who came in to take the class for one day and ended up staying the rest of the year.

Teachers who are away for less than a week usually leave day plans for each day or e-mail them in. Teachers who are away for longer than a week usually don't leave day plans. Of course, there are always exceptions to the rule. The point is that you may have to do some planning and photocopying. Don't roll your eyes at me when I mention the photocopy machine. I threaten to unplug it and plug it back in if it doesn't cooperate. I pray prayers of blessing over it when a red light starts flashing at me. And if I have to change the toner or it shows a paper jam and

I just can't find it, I go straight to the school secretary, who always knows what to do better than anyone else!

Planning for two days or a week is similar to planning for covering a maternity leave or sick leave. You can get help from the teacher if he/she is available, from another teacher, or even from the students. You are not required to prepare detailed lesson plans, complete with page numbers, from the curriculum documents. If you can simply go on with what the students have been learning, that's great! Teach the next page in the math textbook, the next science lesson, etc.

At this point, it's important to remember balance. You can stay at school for three hours, planning lessons; but this is not really necessary. You need to make sure you have planned enough that students have a good lesson, understand the work, and have enough work to fill the time. If the job turns into a longer job, then you can spend three hours figuring out what they have and haven't done, what they need to do, where the resources are, etc.

Students will often be disappointed their teacher is not back the next day and they can show this pretty clearly. But remember that they are happy you are back and that they don't have to get to know another substitute teacher. Although they may not show it, your being there does make their day easier. They already know you and they know what to expect and how you work. Just by agreeing to come back the next day, you have made their day better. And you have some fun tricks up your sleeve and they will enjoy it when you make the effort to help them have fun during the day.

Covering a Maternity/Sick Leave

Congratulations! You were hired to cover a maternity leave, a sick leave, a they-won't-tell-you-why-the-teacher-left-and-you're-a-bit-worried leave. That's great —a long-term occasional job! Well…what are you going to do? No, really, what are you going to do? I recommend not letting panic set in after the euphoria subsides. Did you miss this class in teacher's college—the one where they teach you how to take over a behavioral Grade 8 class halfway through the year? Me too.

Or perhaps you are a retired teacher who only does day-to-day substitute teaching and only in the school where you used to work. One of the teachers who is your good friend begged you to take her class while she had to go look after her mother. Against your better judgment, you agreed. You are a good and kind person! I recommend not letting dread set in after the empathy has long since passed. I mean, I have a mom too—but really!

So the principal takes you to your classroom. You find that the previous teacher left a half-eaten sandwich in the desk, but no pencils, pens, tape, or scissors. The art cupboard has mouse droppings in it and nothing else. You can't find long-term plans or marks; you don't know what the students have already learned or what they need to learn the rest of the year. There are two new students who don't have desks yet; they've been there for two weeks and have been using the teacher's desk. There are no notebooks, erasers, or staples left (although there are three staplers, all with different room numbers written on the top) and the budget for the year has been used up already.

You think I'm exaggerating, don't you?

First things first: take coffee to the caretaker. You will be needing a lot of help and the caretaker is the one who will help you with anything involving furniture and repairs. It's always a good idea to be on good terms with this person. Introduce yourself, give him/her the coffee, chat for five minutes, smile, and say, "See you later." The next day, go again, and take the list of 100 things you need.

It's a good idea to quickly get on the caretaker's good side. It's pretty easy: be friendly but not over-chatty, listen, and make sure the students clean up the classroom for two minutes before they leave the class every day. If you are friendly and your classroom is always clean, the caretaker will like you. If your classroom is messy, the caretaker will not like you, no matter how many cookies you bring! The caretaker can fix something in your classroom quickly...or not. The caretaker can clean up a mess quickly...or not. Having students pick up garbage off the floor every day can be the difference between having blinds that work properly and having a hot, sunny room every afternoon, or the difference between the hole in the wall being quickly fixed and little furry visitors leaving their calling cards (i.e., mouse droppings) every night. Be nice to the caretakers! Ditto for the school secretary: she/he will be giving you as much or more help than the caretaker.

Often teachers going on a long-term leave will leave about a week's worth of plans for the teacher coming in. They also often leave their long-term plans and their e-mail address so you can contact them if you have questions. If they are called away on a family emergency, however, there may be nothing and no way to contact them. In this case, other teachers, an EA, or the principal may know what that class has covered already that year. If worse comes to worst, you can always ask one of the more responsible students (they are easy to pick out: they sit down when you ask and read quietly when you ask; they do not throw bits of erasers at the back of other students' heads). These students will tell you what has been covered and what hasn't.

Now this part I know you learned in teacher's college—you go to the curriculum to see what needs to be taught. You follow the long-term plan provided or you make your own. Schools often provide a mentor teacher for new teachers who can help with your long-term plans. If a mentor is not offered, it's always a good idea to ask if there is anyone who would be willing to mentor you. Once the long-term plan is done, you can figure out which units you will be doing and lesson plans for each lesson in the unit. I always (okay, not always, but almost always) start each lesson with something fun: a story or a game or something to help the students get excited about learning, or at least to stop them from falling asleep! Repeat the above steps for every subject you are teaching. See? Easy-peasy!

Sometimes you are hired to cover a long-term leave and are asked to start the next day. If the teacher has left some plans for a few days, this is okay. If not, on the first day use the lesson plans in this book. While students are working—quietly, because you bribed them with the promise of free time—figure out what you will do the next day and, if there is time, for the rest of the week. It often takes teachers a couple of weeks to get everything organized and planned when taking over a classroom. Principals don't (usually) expect you to have everything worked out that first day. Principals are usually willing to allow you to buy some things (pencils, paper, staples), even if the budget has been all used up for the year. There's no harm in asking. Parents also are often willing to help out when asked and will send in tissue, pencils, etc.

Some long-term occasional teaching jobs can be more difficult than you were expecting them to be—especially the first one. This is a common experience. The students don't listen, you can't find where the teacher left anything, the students won't listen, the lights are broken, the students won't listen. Did I mention the students won't listen? Did you wonder why the teacher took a stress leave? This is where other teachers can be a great support. Talk to the gym teacher, the music teacher, the teacher that taught these students last year. Ask them what they did that worked, tips for helping certain students, how to not go crazy. Even experienced teachers do this with more difficult classes. Just a note: be careful not to complain too much about the class, as this can lead the principal to not ask you to come back to cover another leave.

This is the time to figure out your own style. Try lots of different things and see what works for you. How much noise are you comfortable with in class? Do you want the class sitting in groups or rows? Will you go in before class to prepare or stay after school? Will you use songs or games, or both, or neither? They say it takes about five years to get your own classroom management style. I think it took me about eight years.

The first time you have your own classroom, it can seem to take over your life. You're at school so much, your spouse wonders if you're having an affair with the librarian. Especially when you say you're at school working and then bring work home! It's a good idea to set boundaries for yourself: for example, *I will go to work at 8 a.m. and come home at 6 p.m. and only do one hour of marking at home.* The work really is never-ending. As a teacher, you'll find there is always more you could do, more you should do, and more you'd like to do. It's important to make boundaries so you will still love your job—and your spouse!

There will be days when you want to quit. It just doesn't seem worth it. This teaching thing takes more time and emotional energy than you thought! Hang in there—it does get better! When you want to quit—or maybe just shoot one of the students—it may be time to take a sick day (or a mental health day to avoid sick days). This is when you will find out what a difference you are making in the class. When you come back, the students will ask you why you were away and ask you not to be away again and tell you what a horrible substitute teacher they had (she/he obviously hasn't read this book!). That's when you know you are their beloved teacher—even if they don't say it out loud!

How to Get a Permanent Job by Making Everyone Happy

In case I haven't convinced you that my choice of career should also be your choice of career, here are some tips to getting hired permanently by becoming everyone's favorite substitute. Of course, you can always get a job teaching French. Oops! You didn't study French—too late. You should have listened to your Grade 7 French teacher after all!

Make the Students Happy

Teachers and principals will invite back substitute teachers the students like. They will be impressed that the teacher is able to handle the class and still have students like them. This is actually quite rare. Use all the tips in this book.

Make the Absent Teacher Happy

If you want to be asked back to a school, you have to be liked not only by the kids, but also by the teacher for whom you are substituting. This means that most of the kids actually have to do the work that's been left. I give incentives to the first two or three students who finish to encourage this. I try as much as possible to do what the teacher has left for them to do. Remember: if you want to be asked back, it's best if the note says that you did all the work and the students behaved well. You don't have to outright lie, but I would leave a bad note only if I already knew the teacher or if I didn't care if I returned to that school.

Sometimes it is really hard to understand what the day plans mean; some teachers think substitute teachers are mind readers. Then there's the teacher who doesn't leave the DVD player and TV, just the DVD; or the teacher who assigns a page that doesn't exist in the textbook; etc. Make sure the classroom is left neat and clean. Make sure the classroom is clean—this bears repeating. If not, the caretaker will complain to the administration, who will tell the teacher, and then all three are not happy with you. Make sure that students don't touch anything they aren't supposed to touch; e.g., musical instruments, drama props, the teacher's computer, etc.

Make the Other Teachers Happy

Other teachers may ask you to be flexible as well; perhaps you were supposed to switch classes with someone who now needs their own class for that period. It is good to be flexible because that other teacher may use you as a substitute some day. Also, when it comes time to hire someone permanently, they want someone who fits into the school culture. So when you go to a school, don't sit by yourself at lunch. When you go into the lunchroom, ask to sit at a table with an empty seat. Enter into the conversation—be friendly. Don't take over the conversation, just contribute. Remember small details and ask the teachers about it when you see them later; e.g., "So, did your car give you any more trouble?"

If you have been asked back to a school quite a bit and you like it there, take Timbits in one day for the staff. Leave a thank-you note with your name. It's always nice to be appreciated and it's always nice to eat small, sugary donuts!

Make the Vice-Principal and Principal Happy

Come on time. Don't buzz the office or send anyone to the office. Pick up half-day jobs at your favorite schools. Go in when you had planned to take a day off and they call you at 8:45 a.m.

Make the School Secretaries Happy

School secretaries are often the ones who put the jobs into the computer system. They know which substitute teachers are good and who to call at a moment's notice. It is really, really good to get on the secretary's good side! So, come on time. Wait patiently for their attention, as they are crazy busy in the morning taking messages from parents whose children are pretending to be sick that day. Fill out the attendance properly. Nothing is worse than having the secretary call a parent to ask why their child isn't in school that day, having the parent panic, and then finding out it was just that the attendance was filled out wrong. And for goodness sake, don't fill out the attendance wrong twice! Be flexible and willing to change jobs if they ask.

Make Yourself Happy

This won't get you a job; it just keeps you sane. I guess being sane does help you to get a job...

If the job is too far away, you don't have to pick it up. If they neglected to say it was going to be a French immersion music job, you don't have to go to that school again. If the students swear at you and then swear at the principal and walk away, you don't have to go there again. This is one of the great, great things about substitute teaching—you have choice.

Is This What My Career Is Supposed to Look Like?

I became a substitute teacher in the public school board after being a permanent teacher overseas for two years and then teaching in a private school for two years. I taught day to day for a month or so before becoming a regular substitute teacher in two or three schools. After six months, I started covering a maternity leave. A year later, when that teacher decided not to come back to teaching, I was hired permanently. I was a permanent teacher for two-and-a-half years before I went back to substitute teaching, as it suited my lifestyle more than being a permanent teacher. See? Your career doesn't look quite so bad and complicated now, does it?

Often teachers just graduating will substitute teach for a while before finding a permanent position. Some boards require teachers to have a certain amount of substitute experience before becoming a permanent teacher. How long new graduates substitute teach depends on many factors, including how many teachers are looking for jobs, if they have any training in skills that are needed (e.g., French, music, special education, juggling—you never know...), and plain, old-fashioned luck; i.e., being in the right place at the right time.

Sometimes a teacher finds that substitute teaching suits his/her lifestyle (just like I did) due to a family situation or personality. These teachers have a career in substitute teaching. They often have a small handful of schools where they work most days. In fact, many substitute teachers teach in only one school. These teachers often live across the road or right down the street from that school!

Others have been permanent teachers and decide to do substitute teaching because they have retired or because they are really, really tired of doing report cards. I mean really, how many times can you say that a child is too chatty without saying it outright? "Kaylee needs to work on her listening skills" really means "Kaylee talks too much"!!

Substitute teachers often have another job. Some new teachers continue to work part-time at the job they had in university until they are working enough as a substitute teacher that they can afford to leave that job. Other teachers are self-employed or have another job and enjoy the flexibility of substitute teaching. There used to be a fireman who would substitute teach at one of the schools where I worked. One day in June, word came down the hallway that he was wearing shorts that day. Many of the female teachers made their way up to say hello to him that morning.

No matter what your situation, it's important to remember that no two careers are exactly alike. There is no one right way to do it. Sometimes it's difficult not to compare careers; however, whenever I find myself doing it, it seems I never come out on top. It's important to find what works for you and to do that. If you would like to find a permanent job and it seems to be taking a long, long while, remember that there are others who have waited longer than you. There is always someone. It's important not to get discouraged—and to have good friends who will drink with you when you do!

Advantages to Substitute Teaching

You didn't get a permanent job. You went to 105 interviews in the spring and summer and came in second 104 times (the 105th time you forgot what you were applying for in the interview and thought you'd had an interview with this principal before but couldn't remember). You'd even settle for a special education long-term occasional job at this point—for which you have no training.

I admit it—it's difficult when it feels like all you're doing is baby-sitting and that some fourteen-year-old with braces could do a better job. You want to teach to make a difference in kids' lives; that is difficult to do when you see different students every day. However, you do make a difference. Often the day there is a substitute teacher is a bad one for the students because they get yelled at a lot. When you go in and have fun, it makes a big difference, and you can tell by the way the students want you to be their substitute teacher next time.

I'd like to point out the many advantages to substitute teaching over regular teaching. It's really not as bad as you think.

No Paperwork

No planning, no marking, no recording, no reporting! Paperwork is the part most teachers dislike most. Some days, doing report cards is enough to drive any teacher to become a substitute teacher! Not to mention individual education plans, direct reading assessments, accident/incident reports, permission forms, field-trip forms, letters home about science projects, letters home about inappropriate touching at school, letters home about chicken pox in your classroom, planning for tomorrow, planning for the next unit, planning for the year, planning for the volleyball practice tomorrow, marking math, marking journals, marking spelling, taking all the marks and coming up with a calculation to make a report card mark that's fair, etc., etc., etc.! As a substitute teacher, you don't do any paperwork. All you do is work with students. This is what teachers want—to work with students.

Flexibility

You can take a day off anytime you want, including going on vacation to Cuba during the off-season for $500. Of course, you don't get paid, but—come on—$500! How can you pass it up?

Of course, I always told the kids I never had a student I didn't like. I had students whose behavior I didn't like, who I gave many, many detentions to, but who I liked in theory.

You can say yes or no to any job. (Of course saying no too much is counterproductive...) You can choose the area of the city where you would like to work. If you don't want to go back to a school because you had a horrible experience with students and the administration wasn't supportive, you don't go back. If you don't like the kids, you get to leave at the end of the day (as a permanent teacher, you would have a lot longer wait to get rid of them).

If you want to focus on a certain grade level or subject, you can become known for that over time. You can be the go-to guy for dance and drama or for Kindergarten. For a while, I was substitute teaching music two to three days a week.

Flexibility is one of the best things about substitute teaching. Take advantage of it and don't feel bad!

Exploration

You get to know the city and short cuts to everywhere and how to avoid traffic. You get to know the schools in your city or neighborhood, the principals, teachers, and students. You get to know where is a good place to work and where isn't.

One way to explore schools is by eating lunch in the staff room. The good schools have teachers who will welcome you and talk to you over lunch. The teachers at those schools don't only talk shop over lunch but branch out to sports, current events, family life, movies, TV, and a variety of other topics that are not "Is always-talks-in-a-very-loud-voice-Jonathan in your class this year?"

It is also good to explore the school atmosphere, which is set by the principal. Really difficult schools can turn around with a good principal; even the best school can be intolerable with a bad principal. It's always better to choose to work with a better principal than at a better school. Of course, principals move around every few years if you can last it out. If you substitute teach at a school and you like the principal and she likes you, you can always substitute at her new school when she moves.

You get to find out what age groups and subjects you like. You can try teaching Kindergarten even if you've been a junior–intermediate teacher your whole career. You can teach art and classes with students who are nonverbal. It was while I was substitute teaching that I really came to like intermediate students. I was a primary–junior teacher with a specialty in Kindergarten. But I started enjoying the intermediates' sense of humor. They got sarcasm, which is completely lost on Kindergarten students, let me tell you!

You can try out different classroom management strategies and see what works for you. You can try lots of different ideas, things that you never tried before. In a regular class, you can't keep changing day to day—the kids would freak!

The Hours

School is usually seven hours per day. As a substitute teacher, you are usually teaching five to five-and-a-half hours per day. You start around 8:30 a.m. and leave around 3:30 p.m. You don't take home any work. You don't stay after school for basketball practice. When you're done, you're done.

The Pay

It really is good pay for what amounts to five hours of work per day. Of course, it's not good enough pay for teaching some classes! You know you're in trouble when the secretary warns you that it's a "challenging" class or has "interesting" students. Make sure you find out where the buzzer for the office is!

It's the end of the summer by the time the employment insurance application gets approved, by which time you've maxed out your credit cards on luxuries like food and gas. So apply early.

You get employment insurance in the summer. It's not as good money, but as long as you plan a bit for it, it's okay.

Easy Days

Some days are just really, really easy. The person you are covering for left a movie and the class is watching quietly and you get a lot of reading done. The students have holiday assemblies or scientists in the school or something else for which you don't have to do very much. There is an EA and a volunteer in the classroom and they know the routine, so you pretty much watch them do the work. The school has you in "just in case" they need you, but they end up not needing you and so you have a quiet day in the library.

There are many advantages to substitute teaching. So, when you have a really bad day, just remember that you can go to Italy or France on a trip anytime you want. Perhaps picturing this trip will also help…

Common Questions

Q: Who is my boss?
A: No one principal is your boss, so it's difficult to know who your boss is. The principal you have that day is your boss. The Board of Education is also your boss. The teacher's union is not your boss; however, they can help with many issues, including answering questions about payroll, sick leave, your responsibilities, etc.

Q: How do I know if I'm doing a good job or not?
A: The principals of the schools where you work will let you know if you are doing a good job, if you ask. However, they may not be able to give a lot of feedback until you have been at that school a few times. If schools ask you back, if you become a regular at a school, then you know you are doing a good job. This takes a while. It does not always happen right away. Teachers may also start asking you to come back to their classrooms; this also means you are doing a good job. Finally, students may ask you to come back. This means either that you are doing a good job or that your incentives are working!

Acknowledgments

Thank God, the book is done! There are many people to thank.

I went into teaching to help children. I sincerely hope this book makes a difference in the lives of many students. To the many schools where I have been a regular short-term or long-term substitute, thank you to the administration, staff, and students – I have learned so, so much from you: Brimwood, Clairlea, Maryvale, General Brock, Ionview, Samuel Hearne, and Wexford, among others.

I've spoken with many substitute teachers over the years who came to my sessions or were referred to me and called to talk about their careers. They told me what is really needed by substitute teachers today. Rebekah Ariss, Dayna Dixon, Laura Leet, Marianna Rankin, and others, thank you for sharing. I hope this book answers many of your questions and helps you enjoy your career.

Thank you to Mary Macchiusi and Pembroke Publishers for seeing the value and believing in the book. Thank you to Kat Mototsune for being an excellent editor and for patiently answering all my many questions.

As I am not an expert on every single grade and subject area, thank you to the many teachers I consulted with, including Lisa Bradley, Ranald McKechnie, Rebecca Purvis, Dionne Taylor, and others.

Thank you to Denise Schon and Linsday Dwarka for lending me their expertise in the publishing and editorial process. I would not have got to this point (and would have been much more stressed out) were it not for your help.

As my drawings of cars look a lot like cows, thank you to Katie Cocker and Nadine Foskin for providing diagrams.

Qing Huang, thank you for designing the website where teachers can go to find more tips, videos, and stories about substitute teaching: amandayuill.com

Everyone should have a brother like Mathieu Yuill. Thanks go to him for connecting me with the right people, filming videos, managing the website, and all the advice along the way.

And finally, as the music plays and they drag me off the stage, thank you to my parents Pat and John, my sister Cindy, and family and friends for your love, listening ears, good advice, and encouragement. Thank you, Zola Landu, for your love and support. God knows, I've needed all the help I could get!

Recommended Resources

Websites

Education World, Substitute Survival: Tools You Can Use
http://www.educationworld.com/a_curr/curr260.shtml
• advice, tips, lesson plans, songs, games, and activities

A Packet for Substitute Teachers
http://www.teacherneedhelp.com/students/subtch.htm
• riddles, puzzles, tests, and advice for Grades 1–6.

Super Substitute Teachers
http://www.supersubstituteteachers.com/tips.htm
• resources for substitute and occasional teachers

teAchnology, Substitute Teaching: An Insiders View
http://www.teach-nology.com/tutorials/teaching/sub/
• lesson plans, work sheets, and problem-solving advice

Books

Bowers, Trent (nd) *From Survive to Thrive: What Great Substitute Teachers Do Differently*. http://www.worthington.k12.oh.us/cms/lib02/OH01001900/Centricity/Domain/57/hr_ebook.pdf
• a system to become a successful substitute teacher

Kelley, W. Michael (2003) *Rookie Teaching for Dummies*. Toronto, ON: Wiley.
• find your instructional style and make learning fun

Nelson, Patty (1986) *Teacher's Bag of Tricks: 101 Instant Lessons for Classroom Fun!* Incentive Publications.
• reproducibles and instant ideas for many subjects

Parry, Michael (2006) *100 Ideas for Supply Teachers: Primary School Edition*. London, UK: Bloomsbury.
• activities to keep pupils on task

Pressman, Barbara (2007) *Substitute Teaching from A to Z*. Columbus, OH: McGraw-Hill Education.
• a comprehensive guide by a veteran teaching expert

Index

absent teacher, 149–150
academic tendencies
    Grade 1 students, 44–45
    Grade 2 students, 47
    Grade 3 students, 49
    Grade 4 students, 72
    Grade 5 students, 74
    Grade 6 students, 76
    Grade 7 students, 102
    Grade 8 students, 104
    Kindergarten students, 29
accidents, 44
activity centres, 34
advantages, 152–154
aerodynamics, 79
afternoon,
    getting students to do work, 17–18
    intermediate grades, 110
    junior grades, 83–84
    Kindergarten, 34–35
    primary grades, 55
aggression, 101
airplane graphic, 79
all about you, 14–15
applying to schools, 145
approval, 76
art activities, 138–139
    intermediate activities, 111
    lesson plan, 138–139
    junior grades, 85–86,
    primary grades, 57
    teaching tips, 138
attendance, 23
    art, 139
    behavior (classroom)
      management, 15

dance, 135
drama, 137
French, 128
intermediate grades, 106, 110
junior grades, 78, 83
Kindergarten, 32, 34
music, 133
physical education, 130
primary grades, 50–51
attention
    getting, 9–10, 45
    Grade 1, 44, 45
    Grade 2, 48
    Grade 3, 49–50
    Kindergarten, 30
    tools for keeping, 10–15

balance, 147
ball/name game, 59
bar graph, 109
behavior (classroom) management
    attendance, 15
    office (sending children to), 18
    problem students, 15
    recess problems, 18
    talking, 16
    touching, 16
    work, 17–18
being first, 15, 44, 49
being taken advantage of, 25
belonging, 72
Bingo, 128
Bip/Bop, 59
boundaries
    setting, 103, 149
    testing, 30

boys vs. girls, 111–112

calendar, 32
candy, 11
career, 151–152
caretakers, 147–148
cell phones, 106
Change-up Tag, 130–131
classroom
    cleaning up, 34, 57, 86, 111, 129,
      136, 139, 148
    finding, 21
    management, 15–18
    routines, 23
cliques/clubs, 47
clothing, 20, 22, 28, 57
cloze activities, 51–52, 60–61,
  78–79, 106
complaints, 45–46
computers, 141
counting, 30
crossword, 53–54, 66, 81, 95, 108
crying, 28, 47

Daily Physical Activity (DPA), 17
dance, 134–136
Darling-Won't-You-Please-Smile
  game, 137
dating, 103
day plans/lessons
    art, 138–139,
    dance, 135–136
    drama, 137–138
    finding, 22
    French, 127–129
    intermediate grades, 105–111

junior grades, 77–86
Kindergarten, 31–38
music, 133–134
physical education, 130–132
primary grades, 50–57
Disappearing Coin, 12
dismissal, 25
Doggy, Doggy, Who's Got Your Bone?, 58
drama, 136–138
Duck, Duck, Goose, 37–38

Early Childhood Educator (ECE), 30, 34, 140
Educational Assistant (EA), 30, 146
English as a Second Language, 141
entering students, 23
exploration, 153
extra activities/games
intermediate grades, 111–113
junior grades, 86–87
Kindergarten, 37–38
language, 53–54, 64–65, 81, 107–108
primary grades, 53–54, 57–59

fairness, 49
famous movie/story tableau, 138
finding the classroom, 21
finding day plans, 22
finding the school, 21
fitting in, 101–102
flexibility, 21–22, 152–153
forgetting, 15, 30
Four Number 4s, 87
free time, 11–12
French, 127–129
French Word Search, 129, 143–144
friendship, 47, 49, 72, 74, 76, 101–102, 104
funny stories, 14

games, 12
geography, 141
going home
French, 129
intermediate grades, 111
junior grades, 86
Kindergarten, 37
primary grades, 57

Grade 1
day plans/lessons, 50–57
extra activities/games, 58
starting routines, 50–51
student characteristics, 43–45
teaching well, 45–46
Grade 2
day plans/lessons, 50–57
extra activities/games, 58–59
starting routines, 50–51
student characteristics, 46–47
teaching well, 48
Grade 3
day plans/lessons, 50–57
extra activities/games, 59
starting routines, 51
student characteristics, 48–49
teaching well, 49–50
Grade 4
day plans/lessons, 77–86
extra activities/games, 86
starting routines, 78
student characteristics, 71–72
teaching well, 72–73
Grade 5
day plans/lesson, 77–86
extra activities/games, 86–87
starting routines, 78
student characteristics, 73–74
teaching well, 74–75
Grade 6
day plans/lessons, 77–86
extra activities/games, 87
starting routines, 78
student characteristics, 75–76
teaching well, 76–77
Grade 7
day plans/lessons, 105–111
extra activities, 111–112
starting routines, 106
student characteristics, 101–102
teaching well, 102–103
Grade 8
day plans/lessons, 105–111
extra activities, 112–113
starting routines, 106
student characteristics, 103–104
teaching well, 104–105
gross facts, 13, 32, 50–51, 78, 83–84, 106, 110, 128, 130, 133, 135, 137, 139

Groups of 2, 3, 4 game, 133
growing pains, 73
Guess the Word, 87
Guess Who, 112

hall duty, 25
hands up, 30
happiness, 151
helping, 74
high school, 104
history, 141
How to Freak Out Your Mom, 13
humor, 10, 16, 30–31, 45, 48, 74, 76–77, 102, 104–105

I Spy, 38
ignoring students, 18
illness, 28, 44, 46, 71
inappropriate behavior, 46, 48, 71, 73, 103
incentives/rewards, 10, 11–12
Intermediate Cloze Activity, 106, 114–115
Intermediate Crossword, 108, 121
intermediate grades
afternoon routine, 110
art activities, 111
day plans/lessons, 105–111
extra activities/games, 111–113
going home, 111
Grade 7, 101–103, 111–112
Grade 8, 103–105, 112–113
language activities, 106–108
math activities, 108–109
recess, 108, 111
science activities, 110–111
starting routines, 106
Intermediate Language Activity, 107, 116–117
Intermediate Math Sheet, 109, 122–124
Intermediate Science Experiment, 110, 125
Intermediate Word Search, 107, 119–120
Intermediate Writing Activity, 107, 118
introduction, 10
isolation, 18

jokes, 13, 32, 50–51, 78, 83–84, 106, 110, 128, 130, 133, 135, 137, 139
judgment, 104
Junior Cloze Activity, 79, 88–89
Junior Crossword, 81, 95
junior grades
    afternoon routines, 83–84
    art activities, 85–86
    day plans/lessons, 77–86
    extra activities/games, 86–87
    going home, 86
    Grade 4, 71–73, 86
    Grade 5, 73–75, 86–87
    Grade 6, 75–77, 87
    language activities, 78–81
    lunch, 83
    math activities, 81–83
    recess, 81, 85
    science experiment, 84–85
    starting routines, 78
Junior Language Activity, 80, 90–91
Junior Math Sheet, 83, 96–98
Junior Science Experiment, 84, 99
Junior Word Search, 81, 93–94
Junior Writing Activity, 80, 92

Kindergarten
    activity centres, 34
    afternoon routines, 34–35
    day plans/lessons, 31–38
    extra activities/games, 37–38
    going home, 37
    language activities, 32–33
    lunch, 34
    math activities, 35–36
    science activities, 36–37
    snack, 33, 36
    starting routines, 32
    student characteristics, 27–29
    teaching well, 29–31
Kindergarten Language Activity, 33, 39
Kindergarten Math Activity, 35, 40, 41

language activities
    extra, 53–54, 64–66, 81, 93–95, 107–108
    intermediate grades, 106–108
    junior grades, 78–81
    Kindergarten, 32–33

primary grades, 51–54
teaching, 142
last-minute preparation, 23
library, 142
line order, 44
long-term occasional jobs, 147–149
lunch
    art, 139
    dance, 136
    intermediate grades, 110
    junior grades, 83
    Kindergarten, 34
    music, 134
    physical education, 132
    primary grades, 55
lunch duty, 25
lunchroom supervisor, 146

magic tricks, 12–13
making others happy, 149–151
maternity/sick leave, 147–149
math activities
    intermediate grades, 108–109
    junior grades, 81–83
    Kindergarten, 35–36
    primary grades, 54–55
    teaching, 142
moodiness, 75
movement break, 16
Murder Monsters, 58
music, 132–134

networking, 145
numbers, 29

office (sending to), 18
oral play, 28

paperwork, 152
participation, 28–29
peer pressure, 76
permanent jobs, 149–151
physical characteristics
    Grade 1 students, 43–44
    Grade 2 students, 46–47
    Grade 3 students, 48–49
    Grade 4 students, 71,
    Grade 5 students, 73
    Grade 6 students, 75
    Grade 7 students, 101
    Grade 8 students, 103

Kindergarten students, 27–28
physical education, 129–132
pie graph, 109
planning longer jobs, 147
play-fighting, 103
Primary Cloze Activity, 51, 60–61
Primary Crossword, 53, 66
primary grades
    afternoon routines, 55
    art activities, 57
    day plans/lessons, 50–57
    extra activities/games, 57–59
    going home, 57
    Grade 1, 43–46, 58
    Grade 2, 46–48, 58–59
    Grade 3, 48–50, 59
    language activities, 51–54
    lunch, 55
    math activities, 54–55
    recess, 54, 56
    science activities, 55–56
    starting routines, 50–51
    teaching well, 45–46, 48, 49–50
Primary Language Activity, 52, 62
Primary Math Sheet, 54, 67–69
Primary Science Experiment, 56, 70
Primary Word Search, 53, 64–65
Primary Writing Activity, 53, 63
principal, 150
problem students, 15
puberty, 48, 71, 73, 75, 101, 103

quiet (calling for), 16

reading,
    Kindergarten, 29, 34–35
    primary grades, 51
    silent, 32, 51, 78, 106
recess
    art, 139
    dance, 136
    duty, 20, 25
    intermediate grades, 108, 111
    junior grades, 81, 85
    music, 134
    physical education, 132
    primary grades, 54, 57
    problems, 18
relationship building, 9
repetition, 46
reporting students, 18

resolving issues, 49
résumé and cover letter, 145
ripped-paper picture, 139
Rock, Paper, Scissors tournament, 86
routines,
    classroom, 23
    Kindergarten, 32

scary stories, 13–14
schedules, 30
school, finding, 21
science activities
    intermediate grades, 110–111
    junior grades, 84–85
    Kindergarten, 36–37
    primary grades, 55–56
    teaching, 142
secretaries, 150
self-introduction, 23
    art, 139
    dance, 135
    drama, 137
    French, 128
    intermediate grades, 106
    junior grades, 78
    Kindergarten, 32
    music, 133
    physical education, 130
    primary grades, 50–51
Seven Up, 86
show and tell, 35
sideline soccer, 132
Silent Ball, 86–87
silent reading, 32, 51, 78, 106
singing,
    Grade 1, 45, 58
    Grade 2, 58
    Kindergarten, 30, 37
    music, 132
Sleeping Beauty, 58
slow times, 146
snack (Kindergarten), 33, 36
soccer
    sideline, 132
    tournament, 131–132

social studies, 141
social tendencies
    Grade 1 students, 44
    Grade 2 students, 47
    Grade 3 students, 49
    Grade 4 students, 72
    Grade 5 students, 74
    Grade 6 students, 75–76
    Grade 7 students, 101–102
    Grade 8 students, 104
    Kindergarten students, 28–29
special education, 140
special helper, 32
starting routines
    intermediate grades, 106
    junior grades, 78
    Kindergarten, 32
    primary grades, 50–51
stickers, 11
stomach aches, 71
Stomp routine, 135–136
stories
    art, 139
    dance, 135
    drama, 137
    French, 128
    funny, 14
    intermediate grades, 106
    junior grades, 78, 83–84
    Kindergarten, 32, 34
    music, 133
    physical education, 130
    primary grades, 50–51
    scary, 13–14
    tableau, 137
style, 19, 149

T-chart, 108
tableau, 137, 138
talking (quieting students), 16
teaching other subjects, 139–142
teaching well
    Grade 1, 45–46
    Grade 2, 48
    Grade 3, 49–50
    Grade 4, 72–73

Grade 5, 74–75
Grade 6, 76–77
Grade 7, 102–103
Grade 8, 104–105
Kindergarten, 29–31
toilet training, 28
tools
    all about you, 14–15
    funny stories, 14
    gross facts, 13
    incentives/rewards, 11–12
    jokes, 13
    magic tricks, 12–13
    scary stories, 13–14
    what to take with you, 20
tooth loss, 28, 43, 48–49
touching, 16
    Grade 1, 44
    Grade 8, 103
    Kindergarten, 27–28, 29
True or False, 112
turning down jobs, 146
Two Truths and a Lie, 87
typical day
    before students arrive, 21–23
    with students, 23–25

vice-principal, 150
volunteering, 145

Where's the Coin, 12
withdrawing privileges, 18
word search, 53, 64–65, 107
work
    doing work left by teacher, 24
    getting students to do work, 17–18
    taking up work, 24
Would You Rather…?, 112–113
writing activities
    intermediate grades, 107
    junior grades, 80–81
    Kindergarten, 29
    primary grades, 53

yard duty, 20, 25